STUDY GUIDE

HOW TO FIGHT RACISM

STUDY GUIDE

TEN SESSIONS

Courageous Christianity and the
Journey toward Racial Justice

JEMAR TISBY

WITH BETH GRAYBILL

ZONDERVAN
REFLECTIVE

ZONDERVAN REFLECTIVE

How to Fight Racism Study Guide
Copyright © 2021 by Jemar Tisby

Published in Grand Rapids, Michigan, by Zondervan. Zondervan is a registered trademark of The Zondervan Corporation, L.L.C., a wholly owned subsidiary of HarperCollins Christian Publishing, Inc.

Requests for information should be addressed to customercare@harpercollins.com.

Zondervan titles may be purchased in bulk for educational, business, fundraising, or sales promotional use. For information, please email SpecialMarkets@Zondervan.com.

ISBN 978-0-310-17432-5 (softcover)

ISBN 978-0-310-11323-2 (ebook)

Cover Design: Faceout Studio
Cover Photo: Shutterstock
Interior Design: Kait Lamphere

Printed in the United States of America

24 25 26 27 28 29 30 31 32 33 34 /TRM/ 16 15 14 13 12 11 10 9 8 7 6 5 4 3 2 1

CONTENTS

Introduction vii
How to Use This Guide ix

Session 1: How to Fight Racism 1

PART 1: Awareness
Session 2: How to Explain Race and the Image of God 14
Session 3: How to Explore Your Racial Identity 32
Session 4: How to Study the History of Race 49

PART 2: Relationships
Session 5: How to Do Reconciliation Right 66
Session 6: How to Make Friends 84
Session 7: How to Build Diverse Communities 100

PART 3: Commitment
Session 8: How to Work for Racial Justice 117
Session 9: How to Fight Systemic Racism 133
Session 10: How to Orient Your Life to Racial Justice 150
Conclusion 169

Closing Words 175
Leader's Guide 177

INTRODUCTION

Hello, friend! Welcome to the *How to Fight Racism Study Guide*. This guide, which includes ten teaching sessions and a conclusion, is meant to be a companion learning experience to my book, *How to Fight Racism*, and its video study. There is a growing swell of people who recognize the fierce sense of urgency when it comes to fighting racism. The pages of the book contain my answer to the most frequent question I receive about fighting racism: *"What do we do?"* This study guide and accompanying video study are designed to prioritize practical ways to answer that question.

This journey toward racial justice is for those who realize racism is a problem nationwide and worldwide and want to be a part of the solution, but also need guidance about what exactly you could be doing as an individual, a church, a community, or an organization to push back against racism. While I believe the journey is open to all, I am convinced that Christians must show up in this fight against racism. This is what I call *courageous Christianity*. From my point of view, *courageous* Christianity contrasts with the *complicit* Christianity that has led so many religious people to perpetuate racism and cooperate with bigotry instead of challenging it. But racial justice comes from the struggle of those who choose to stand against racism courageously rather than to compromise with it. And now is the time for our fellow Christians to be courageous, to dare to love through action, and to risk everything for the sake of justice.

Here's how I propose we live out courageous Christianity in the face of racial injustice. The book and this study are structured around an important model I created called the ARC of Racial Justice. ARC is an acronym that stands for:

1. Awareness
2. Relationships
3. Commitment

In this study, you will learn ways to increase your *awareness* by studying history, exploring your personal narrative, and grasping what God says about the dignity of the human person. You will also learn to see that you cannot have true racial justice without developing authentic *relationships* with people who are different from you. And you will learn that building awareness and developing relationships is what enables you to make a *commitment* to dismantle racist attitudes, structures, laws, and policies—starting with your heart and moving out to the systems and structures of our nation and our world. This model is grounded in the head-hands-heart metaphor with *awareness* as the head, *relationships* as the heart, and *commitment* as the hands. If we're honest, many of us gravitate toward one part of this model more than the whole. Some of us love to devour information to increase our knowledge and awareness through books, articles, and documentaries. Others forge admirable relationships with people from a wide spectrum of backgrounds and experiences. Still others are activists on the front lines of protests and leading campaigns for radical change. While each response is noble, a holistic response to racial justice *must* include all three aspects: *awareness*, *relationships*, and *commitment*.

The ARC of Racial Justice provides helpful shorthand for a comprehensive approach to racial justice and race reforms. But the point of the model is not to keep all actions equal in number; rather, the goal is to keep all three areas of *awareness*, *relationships*, and *commitment* in conversation and tension with one another. This ensures that no person or organization focuses on one area to the exclusion of the other areas. But the three categories interact in a dance that changes cadence and rhythm according to the music of the moment. This model is not linear, meaning you will not progress from *awareness* to *relationships* to *commitment*—that sounds more like a recipe than a dance. My hope is you will grow in each area, knowing at times that one racial justice practice will build your capacity to fight racism in multiple areas of life.

Here is the truth: the process of growing in *awareness*, *relationships*, and *commitment* never ends. Racial justice is a journey without a finish line, and fighting racism is an ongoing series of steps and stops along the way. Not all of us will have the same starting point or the same speed on this journey. But the eventual destination is crucial: *racial equity and justice for all people of every racial and ethnic background*. This is where harmony and unity will prevail in the midst of diversity. And I believe success on this journey is defined by the actions we take rather than the results we achieve. Let's begin this journey together.

Jemar Tisby

HOW TO USE THIS GUIDE

The *How to Fight Racism Video Study* is designed to be experienced in a group setting such as a Bible study, Sunday school class, or any small group gathering. Each session begins with a welcome section, two questions or reading suggestions to get you thinking about the topic. You will then watch a video with Jemar Tisby and engage in some small-group discussion. You will close each session with a time of prayer as a group.

Each person in the group should have his or her own copy of this study guide and a Bible. Multiple translations will be used throughout the study, so whatever translation you have is fine. You are also encouraged to have a copy of the *How to Fight Racism* book, as reading the book alongside the curriculum will provide you with deeper insights and make the journey more meaningful, especially for your community context. (See the "For Next Week" section at the end of each between-studies section for the chapters in the book that correspond to material you and your group are discussing.)

To get the most out of your group experience, keep the following points in mind. First, the real growth in this study will happen during your small-group time. This is where you will process the content of the teaching for the week, ask questions, and learn from others as you hear what God is doing in their lives as they journey toward racial justice. For this reason, it is important for you to be fully committed to the group and attend each session so you can build trust and rapport with the other members. If you choose to only go through the motions, or if you refrain from participating, there is less of a chance you will find what you're looking for during this study.

Second, remember the goal of your small group is to serve as a place where people can share, learn about God and racial justice, build intimacy and friendship, and make a commitment to live as courageous Christians. For this reason, seek to make your group a safe place. This means being honest about your thoughts and feelings and listening carefully to everyone else's opinion.

(If you are a group leader, there are additional instructions and resources in the back of the book for leading a productive discussion group.)

Third, resist the temptation to fix a problem someone might be having or to correct his or her theology, as that's not the purpose of your small-group time. Also, keep everything your group shares confidential. This will foster a rewarding sense of community in your group and create a place where people can heal, be challenged, and grow spiritually.

Following your group time, reflect on the material you've covered by engaging in a between-sessions activity that includes additional *essential understandings* and *racial justice practices*. For each session, you may wish to complete the personal study all in one sitting or spread it out over a few days (for example, working on it for fifteen minutes a day on different days that week). Note that if you are unable to finish (or even start!) your between-sessions personal study, you should still participate in the group study teaching session. You are still wanted and welcomed in the conversation even if you don't have your "homework" done.

Keep in mind that the videos, discussion questions, and activities are meant to kick-start your journey so you are not only open to what God wants you to hear about racial justice but also how to apply the practices to your life. As you go through this study, be open and listen to what God is saying to you as you discover a healthy, courageous perspective on *How to Fight Racism*.

Note: If you are a group leader, there are additional resources provided in the back of this guide to help you lead your group members through the study.

HOW TO FIGHT RACISM

Civil rights is often seen in social and political terms.
We often fail to recognize this movement as one of the most
significant faith-based campaigns in American history.
—SOON-CHAN RAH

Welcome

Welcome to session 1 of *How to Fight Racism*. The fact that you are here, listening to this teaching, meeting online or in-person as a group, and answering these questions means you're willing to be part of this movement as we journey toward racial justice. The goal of this journey is for all of us to be better equipped in the fight against racism and take the necessary next steps toward equity and justice. I often hear people asking if racism is mostly a matter of personal attitudes and actions or if it's the result of systemic structures and institutional policies. And my answer is, *it's both*. Just look around and read the news. Racial justice must occur at both the individual and institutional levels. W. E. B. DuBois once said, "The cost of liberty is less than the price of repression," and when that becomes true for you, then you will be ready to take the next steps toward racial justice. Now, only time will tell if the grassroots efforts to fight racism during the uprisings and protests of 2020 will lead to lasting transformation. But what is clear is that racial progress does not occur apart from the sustained efforts of people who dedicate themselves to fighting racism in all its forms. That's why we're here today. We need another generation of people willing to fight for freedom. We need a movement of people who will not back away in the face of racism and the lie of white supremacy. And I believe the key to fighting racism is by participating in a model I developed and refer to as the *ARC of Racial Justice*. The ARC of Racial Justice includes increasing your *awareness* by studying history, exploring your personal narrative and grasping what God says about the dignity of the human person. It includes learning to see that you cannot have true racial justice without developing authentic *relationships* with people who are different from you. And it is by building awareness and developing relationships that the ARC includes enabling you to make a *commitment* to dismantle racist attitudes, structures, laws, and policies—starting with your heart and moving out to the systems and structures of our nation and our world. As history demonstrates, we can find creative solutions to society's most pressing problems—including racism—when people of goodwill get together and have *hope*. I'm guessing each one of you is carrying a spirit of *hope* today since you decided to show up for this conversation and take a good hard look at racial justice, so let's get started.

Share

If you or any of your group members are just getting to know one another, take a few minutes to introduce yourselves. Then, to kick things off, briefly discuss one of the following statements:

- What sparks the desire for people to see change?
  —*or*—
- How does someone develop a burden to combat racism?

Watch

Play the video segment for session 1. As you watch, use the following outline to record any thoughts or concepts that stand out to you.

Notes

Something Is Different
- George Floyd
- Breonna Taylor

- Ahmaud Arbery
- Christian Cooper

Signs of Change

Racial Justice

> *When people of goodwill get together, they can find*
> *creative solutions to society's most pressing problems.*
> —JEMAR TISBY

What Do We Do?

How to Fight Racism provides the practical aspects of how to fight for racial justice.

The ARC of Racial Justice

- **A**wareness: building our knowledge and understanding about race and racism
- **R**elationships: all racial justice is relational and requires healthy friendships and collaboration in order to be on this journey *together*
- **C**ommitment: it is a commitment to dismantle racist policies and promote policies that provide equity and justice

> *At some point we need to act on a systemic and institutional*
> *level to change racist patterns and practices.*
> —JEMAR TISBY

Considerations about the Arc of Racial Justice

- It's not a linear process.
- It's a never-ending process.

It's not about perfect balance; it's about a dynamic dance.

Racial Justice Is a Journey, Not a Destination

And the goals are:

- racial harmony
- equity
- justice

> *It's about the people we become*
> *along the way and others who*
> *we meet along this path.*
> —JEMAR TISBY

The Progress of Racial Justice

Courageous Christianity

Christians are part of the problem and part of the solution.

Scripture provides a framework for the need and motivation of racial justice.

Prophetic Imagination (Walter Brueggemann) is about imagining ways we can work against racism to promote a future we can all embrace.

The Practices of Racial Justice

- an invitation to dream
- an invitation to imagine possibilities and alternatives beyond what we see
- an invitation to reflect and evaluate before offering criticism

The Structure of the How to Fight Racism *Study*

- ARC: Awareness, Relationships, Commitment
- Essential Understandings
- Racial Justice Practices

Exemplars: As we get started, consider examples of particular individuals who have been fighting racism and taken steps toward racial justice.

> *If I fall, I'll fall five feet and four*
> *inches forward in the fight for*
> *freedom. I'm not backing off.*
> —FANNIE LOU HAMER

Discuss

Take a few minutes with your group members to discuss what you just watched and explore these concepts in Scripture.

1. What stood out to you from Jemar's teaching on how to fight racism?

   _____

   _____

   _____

   _____

2. Provide a specific example of how you have experienced racism or have witnessed racism in the life of someone close to you.

   _____

   _____

   _____

   _____

3. Consider Jemar's ARC of Racial Justice. How do you think we can increase our *awareness* of racial justice?

   _____

   _____

   _____

   _____

4. How can we foster *relationships* in a way that promotes racial justice?

   _____

   _____

   _____

   _____

5. How can we improve our *commitment* to racial justice?

   _____

   _____

   _____

   _____

6. Jemar said Christians have been part of the *problem* and part of the *solution* for racial justice. How have you known this to be true in seeing the response to racism from the Christian community around you?

   _____

   _____

   _____

7. What responsibility do you think Christians have in the fight against racism, and why?

_____

_____

_____

_____

8. What hopes and expectations do you have for yourself, for your group, and for your faith community as you dive into this study over the next ten weeks on _How to Fight Racism_?

_____

_____

_____

_____

Pray

Pray as a group before you close your time together. Ask God to open your hearts and minds and allow you to see the racism around you, maybe even _within_ you. Ask God to give you hope and passion in your pursuit of racial justice. Use this space to keep track of prayer requests and group updates.

_____

_____

_____

_____

_____

_____

_____

_____

_____

_____

_____

_____

_____

BETWEEN-SESSIONS PERSONAL STUDY

Weekly Reflection

Before you begin this between-sessions exercise, briefly review your notes for video session 1. In the space below, write down the *most significant point* you took away from this session.

_____
_____
_____
_____
_____
_____
_____
_____

Diving Deeper: Essential Understandings

As we move forward in this study, we will use this section to explore the essential understandings Jemar brings to our attention in each session, as well as the additional essential understandings found in each chapter of *How to Fight Racism*.

For session 1, the ARC of Racial Justice *is* our essential understanding, in addition to the exemplars we find carrying out justice and fighting racism long before the racial unrest of 2020. Take a few minutes to reflect on these understandings and the corresponding questions.

The ARC of Racial Justice

How essential is the Arc of Racial Justice to your understanding of the need to fight racism?

_____
_____
_____
_____
_____

Using a scale from 1 (least effective) to 10 (most effective), how would you rate yourself in the following areas regarding racism and racial justice:

Awareness: I am aware of racism and the need for racial justice because I frequently study history, explore my own personal narrative, and read the Bible to understand what God says about the dignity of humanity.

| 1 | 2 | 3 | 4 | 5 | 6 | 7 | 8 | 9 | 10 |

How are you specifically doing this?

_____
_____
_____
_____
_____
_____

Relationships: I regularly surround myself and build authentic relationships with people who are different from me.

| 1 | 2 | 3 | 4 | 5 | 6 | 7 | 8 | 9 | 10 |

How are you specifically doing this?

_____
_____
_____
_____
_____

Commitment: I am committed to dismantling racism—the attitudes, structures, laws, and policies—within me, in the systems and structures of my community, and in our nation.

1	2	3	4	5	6	7	8	9	10

How are you specifically doing this?

_____

_____

_____

_____

_____

Now go back and think about how the people around you would rate you according to the ARC of Racial Justice.

Do your aspirations to fight racism line up with your actions? If no, why not? If yes, where are there areas for improvement?

_____

_____

_____

_____

Taking Action: Racial Justice Practices

As we move forward in this study, we will use this section to explore the racial justice practices Jemar brings to our attention in each session, as well as the additional practices found in each chapter of *How to Fight Racism*.

For session 1, our racial justice practice is to consider the exemplars we find carrying out justice and fighting racism long before the racial unrest of 2020. Take a few minutes to reflect on this practice and the corresponding questions:

Exemplars: Who are the individuals that come to mind when you consider courageous Christianity and the long journey of racial justice/ How have they taken courageous steps, informed by faith, to fight racism? Why are these particular individuals meaningful to you?

1. _____ (name)

The courageous steps of faith this person has taken to fight racism:

_____
_____
_____
_____

Why this individual is meaningful to me:

_____
_____
_____
_____
_____

2. _____ (name)

The courageous steps of faith this person has taken to fight racism:

_____
_____
_____
_____

Why this individual is meaningful to me:

_____
_____
_____
_____
_____

3. _____ (name)

The courageous steps of faith this person has taken to fight racism:

_____
_____
_____
_____

Why this individual is meaningful to me:

_____
_____
_____
_____
_____

4. _____ (name)

The courageous steps of faith this person has taken to fight racism:

_____
_____
_____
_____
_____

Why this individual is meaningful to me:

_____
_____
_____
_____
_____

5. _____ (name)

The courageous steps of faith this person has taken to fight racism:

_____
_____
_____
_____
_____

Why this individual is meaningful to me:

_____
_____
_____
_____
_____

Be Specific: Your Next Step

What specific step will you take this week as a result of what you've learned and explored today? Pay attention to the areas where you felt most convicted as you moved through this material. Perhaps there's a specific next step you need to take to lean into the areas of conviction or sensitivity you experienced today. Give yourself a specific due date for your next step. Then take it one step further and share your action step and due date with a friend or colleague. It helps to have accountability in taking the next step.

As a result of what I learned in this session, I will:

_____

_____

_____

_____

_____

And I will do this by:

_____ (date)

Pray

Take a few moments to reflect on what you've learned today and over the course of session 1. Invite God to give you a clear perspective of his love and truth on the journey of racial justice. Ask God if there's a truth he wants you to lean into as you consider the way you model the ARC of Racial Justice and the courageous, faith-filled ways you show up in the world. Use this space to write out your prayer or journal your thoughts.

_____

_____

_____

_____

_____

_____

For Next Week: Read chapter 2 in *How to Fight Racism* and use the space below to write any insights or questions from your personal study that you want to discuss at the next group meeting.

_____
_____
_____
_____
_____
_____
_____

Journal, Reflections, and Notes

_____
_____
_____
_____
_____
_____
_____
_____
_____
_____
_____
_____
_____
_____
_____
_____
_____
_____
_____
_____
_____
_____

HOW TO EXPLAIN RACE AND THE IMAGE OF GOD

But you are a chosen race, a royal priesthood, a holy nation, a people
for his own possession, that you may proclaim the excellencies of
him who called you out of darkness into his marvelous light.

—1 PETER 2:9 ESV

Welcome

Welcome to session 2 of *How to Fight Racism*. In order to fight racism, we must begin by acknowledging that race is an invented category—one that offers certain privileges and advantages to a particular group of people to the detriment of all those who are excluded from that group. In the US context, this means white people have privileges and advantages at the exclusion of "nonwhite" people, or people of color. Race is what we call a "social construct" because it is based on a set of customs and practices—a caste system—that keeps white people in a superior position to people of color through oppression and exploitation. Race has no basis in biological or spiritual reality because it is socially determined. In fact, in the US, race has largely been defined in terms of physical appearance. Yes, you read that right: *race is largely defined by physical appearance in the US*. And while the concept of race has changed over time, the ideology of race remains a potent force in our world today. White people of European descent enjoy greater access to professional opportunities, high-quality education, more financial wealth, the presumption of innocence, and normality. That is why no matter their level of achievement, people of color are situated on the outermost rings of American social circles. But how do we reconcile this reality with the wisdom of Scripture and the dignity given to *all* of humanity by God? Scripture tells us that we do not simply *have* the image of God; we *are* the image of God, thoroughly and holistically, as human beings. This means *all people* equally bear the likeness of God. To get specific, the image of God extends to Black *and* white people, men *and* women, rich *and* poor, incarcerated *and* free, queer *and* straight, documented *and* undocumented, abled *and* disabled, powerful *and* oppressed. God's fingerprints rest upon every single personal without restriction. Each and every one of us bear incalculable and inviolable value, which makes race a problematic issue. In order to fight for racial justice, racism must not be lightly dismissed. It must be treated as the evil offense against God and human beings that it is. So my hope today is that this session expands our awareness of race from a Christian perspective, and that you walk away understanding the foundational beliefs on which many of the racial justice practices are built.

Share

If you or any of your group members are just getting to know one another, take a few minutes to introduce yourselves. Then, to kick things off, briefly discuss one of the following statements:

- What does it mean to be an *image bearer of God*?
  —or—
- How are race and ethnicity similar or different?

Watch

Play the video segment for session 2. As you watch, use the following outline to record any thoughts or concepts that stand out to you.

Notes
The Story of Kip and Alice Rhinelander (1924)

Race Is:

Essential Understandings

1. Race as a Social Construct

Race is technically the amount of melanin (tone) in one's skin.
Race is built on three main ideas:
- Race is elastic.
- Race is built on physical appearance.
- Race has social meaning.

2. Race and the Bible

A. The human race

> *And he said to the human race,*
> *"The fear of the Lord—that is wisdom,*
> *and to shun evil is understanding."*
> —JOB 28:28

B. Race as "genos": a spiritual designation

> *But you are a chosen people, a royal priesthood,*
> *a holy nation, God's special possession, that you*
> *may declare the excellencies of him who called you*
> *out of darkness. and into his marvelous light.*
> —1 PETER 2:9 NASB

C. Ethnicity (Acts 2)

> *The term ethnicity is flexible enough to encompass*
> *language, nation of origin and religion.*
> —J. DANIEL HAYS, *FROM EVERY PEOPLE AND*
> *NATION: A BIBLICAL THEOLOGY OF RACE* (2003)

Ethnicity includes differences among various people groups:
- physical appearance
- language
- nation of origin
- religion

3. A Biblical Theology of Race

The unfolding story of race, or in biblical terms, *ethnicity*.

> *Diversity wasn't God's plan B. It was*
> *there right from the beginning.*
> —JEMAR TISBY

Genesis 3: The first gospel or the first announcement of good news.

> *And I will put enmity*
> *between you and the woman,*
> *and between your offspring and hers;*
> *he will crush your head*
> *and you will strike his heel.*
> —GENESIS 3:15

Deliverance and salvation for *all*.

> *I will make you into a great nation,*
> *and I will bless you;*
> *I will make your name great,*
> *and you will be a blessing.*
> *I will bless those who bless you,*
> *and whoever curses you I will curse;*
> *and all peoples on earth*
> *will be blessed through you.*
> —GENESIS 12:2–3

Salvation is not limited to just one group of people.

> *The mountain of the LORD's temple will be established*
> *as the highest of the mountains;*
> *it will be exalted above the hills,*
> *and all nations will stream to it.*
> —ISAIAH 2:2

We all have the opportunity to hear the good news be proclaimed.

> *For my eyes have seen your salvation,*
> *which you have prepared in the sight of all nations:*
> *a light for revelation to the Gentiles,*
> *and the glory of your people Israel.*
> —LUKE 2:30–32

Simeon says that salvation goes to Gentiles, non-Jewish people.

> *But you will receive power when the Holy*
> *Spirit comes on you; and you will be my*
> *witnesses in Jerusalem, and in all Judea*
> *and Samaria, and to the ends of the earth.*
> —ACTS 1:8

The parting command of Jesus is to spread the good news to *all* people.

> *And they sang a new song, saying:*
>
> *"You are worthy to take the scroll*
> *and to open its seals,*
> *because you were slain,*
> *and with your blood you purchased for God*
> *persons from every tribe and language*
> *and people and nation."*
> —REVELATION 5:9

> *After this I looked, and there before me was a great*
> *multitude that no one could count, from every nation,*
> *tribe, people and language, standing there before the*
> *throne and before the Lamb. They were wearing white*
> *robes and were holding palm branches in their hands.*
> —REVELATION 7:9

Eternity will be multiethnic. *If that's going to be true then, how do we make it true now?*

COLE AND WALKER, MEMPHIS 1968: THE SANITATION STRIKE

I Am a Man.
—SANITATION WORKERS' SIGNS, 1968

THE BLACK FREEDOM STRUGGLE

Black is Beautiful
I am Somebody
Black Lives Matter

All of these words and phrases are meant
to communicate the humanity and equality
of black people in a society that is built
and rife with white supremacy.
—JEMAR TISBY

4. Imago Dei: *The Image of God*

Then God said, "Let us make mankind in our
image, in our likeness, so that they may rule over
the fish in the sea and the birds in the sky, over
the livestock and all the wild animals, and over
all the creatures that move along the ground."

So God created mankind in his own image,
in the image of God he created them;
male and female he created them.
—GENESIS 1:26–27

THE COHERENT NARRATIVE OF CHRISTIANITY IN THE FIGHT FOR RACIAL JUSTICE
The invaluable existence of all of humanity, made in the image of God.
Being made in the image of God:
- **doesn't** mean we *are* God
- **does** mean we reflect characteristics of God
- **doesn't** mean we are *like* the image of God
- **does** mean we *are* the image of God

- **does** mean we are *all* worthy of dignity and respect in our very being, regardless of our color
- **does** mean we bear the image of God individually *and* collectively

DEFACING THE IMAGE OF GOD ACCORDING TO ETHNICITY
- Printed resources
- Tropes
- Social issues

> *The image of God is a foundational*
> *Christian belief for understanding how*
> *we should interact with one another.*
> **—JEMAR TISBY**

Racial Justice Practices

1. Teach What the Bible Says about Race and Ethnicity

Don't assume you already know how the Bible teaches on these topics.
Tips for teaching:
- Give people lead-up time.
- Do this in groups whenever possible.

2. Learn Theology from the Disinherited

Exercise: Close your eyes and think of five theologians who have shaped your thinking about religion. Now, close your eyes and think about five theologians of color who have shaped your thinking.

Learn from faith communities that aren't in the majority racial group.
Jesus and the Disinherited by Howard Thurman (1996)
Consider how the gospel is "good news" for the marginalized and the oppressed by:
- diversifying your bookshelf
- listening to different pastors and sources
- learning from people who come from marginalized and oppressed groups

3. Treat Racism as It Should Be Considered, a Sin

Do this both inside and outside the church.
Every being has inherent dignity, value, and worth because we are *all* made in the image and likeness of God.

Discuss

Take a few minutes with your group members to discuss what you just watched and explore these concepts in Scripture.

1. What stood out to you from Jemar's teaching on how to explain race and the image of God?

   _____

   _____

   _____

2. According to Jemar, what is the difference between race and ethnicity?

   _____

   _____

   _____

   _____

3. Provide a specific example of how you experienced or witnessed the Black struggle for freedom.

   _____

   _____

   _____

   _____

4. How does your faith inform your view of racial justice and the practices you participate in regarding "liberty and justice for all"?

   _____

   _____

   _____

   _____

5. Review the verses Jemar mentioned in his teaching. Which verse speaks to you most about the inherent value of *all* humans, and why?

   _____

   _____

   _____

   _____

6. How do you engage with fellow Christians who deny the inherent worth and value of other human beings because of the color of their skin or because of their past actions?

_____

_____

_____

7. Who are the theologians who have shaped your thinking about religion? How many of these theologians are women and/or people of color? Who will you specifically seek to learn from them as a result of this realization?

_____

_____

_____

8. Jemar challenged us to consider how the gospel is "good news" for those who have been marginalized and oppressed. What steps will you take to diversify your bookshelf, listen to different pastors and different sources, and learn from marginalized and oppressed groups of people? Be specific on where you will go to find new voices and new sources.

_____

_____

_____

Pray

Pray as a group before you close your time together. Ask God to show you how you've participated in the oppression or exploitation of others, especially people of color, because of your understanding of race. Ask God to help you see your brothers and sisters and fellow humans the way God does—as _image bearers_. Use this space to keep track of prayer requests and group updates.

_____

_____

_____

_____

BETWEEN-SESSIONS PERSONAL STUDY

Weekly Reflection

Before you begin the between-sessions exercises, briefly review your video notes for session 2. In the space below, write down the *most significant point* you took away from this session.

_____

_____

_____

_____

_____

_____

Diving Deeper: Essential Understandings

Reflect on the essential understandings Jemar provided in the video teaching, as well as the additional content for each of these essential understandings found in chapter 2 of *How to Fight Racism*. You may want to review the notes you took during the teaching session regarding each essential understanding as you read the corresponding questions.

1. Race as a Social Construct

This means race is a socially determined category, and it has no basis in spiritual or biological reality. Race is merely an indication of the amount of melanin in one's skin. And the slight variance of melanin found between people of color and white people does not set inherent limits on intelligence, cultural creativity, or social location. Instead, limits have been enacted by one group of people (mostly white people) over another (mostly Black people and other people of color) as individuals and communities make deliberate decisions to hold up one group over others.

What else stood out to you about this essential understanding from Jemar's teaching in the video and from this chapter in *How to Fight Racism*?

_____

_____

_____

_____

_____

_____

_____

_____

_____

_____

_____

_____

How does this understanding change your view of the world around you?

_____

_____

_____

_____

_____

2. Race and the Bible

The Bible translates the word *race* generally in two ways. The first is in reference to the "human race," and this is usually used to emphasize the unified origins of our common humanity. The Bible also uses the term *race* to indicate the difference between those who believe in Jesus Christ as the Messiah and those who do not. In this last instance, the term *race* comes from the Greek word *genos* and does not refer to a person's skin color or other physical features. The word simply designates people who are part of God's new holy nation—the church—through faith in Jesus.

What else stood out to you about this essential understanding from Jemar's teaching in the video and from this chapter in *How to Fight Racism*?

_____

_____

_____

_____

_____

_____

_____

How does this understanding change your view of the world around you?

_____

_____

_____

_____

_____

3. A Biblical Theology of Race

Throughout Scripture God reveals an unfolding plan for ethnic diversity that expands in scope from Genesis to Revelation. God's plan for salvation is built on the presumption of human equality and dignity and always assumes a multiethnic character. Diversity is God's "plan A" for the church. The Christian picture of eternity is multihued, multilingual, multinational, multiethnic fellowship with others in never-ending worship of the triune God (Father, Son, and Holy Spirit). From beginning to end, God has planned for an ethnically diverse church.

What else stood out to you about this essential understanding from Jemar's teaching in the video and from this chapter in *How to Fight Racism*?

_____

_____

_____

_____

_____

_____

_____

_____

How does this understanding change your view of the world around you?

_____
_____
_____
_____
_____

4. *Imago Dei*: The Image of God

In the first chapter of the first book of the Bible, God communicates the essential unity and equality of all people: "'Let us make mankind in our image, in our likeness.' . . . So God created mankind in his own image, in the image of God he created them; male and female he created them" (Gen. 1:26–27). Being made in the image and likeness of God means that human beings hold certain similarities with God. And as God's image bearers, all people have innate dignity and worth. We simply do not *have* the image of God—we *are* the image of God.

What else stood out to you about this essential understanding from Jemar's teaching in the video and from this chapter in _How to Fight Racism_?

_____
_____
_____
_____
_____
_____
_____
_____
_____
_____

How does this understanding change your view of the world around you?

_____
_____
_____
_____
_____

Taking Action: Racial Justice Practices

Now reflect on the racial justice practices Jemar provided in the video teaching, as well as the additional content for each of these practices found in chapter 2 of *How to Fight Racism*. You may want to review the notes you took during the teaching session regarding each racial justice practice as you read the corresponding questions.

1. Teach What the Bible Says about Race and Ethnicity

It is a good idea in the fight against racism to start by teaching what the Bible has to say on the topic. It is not safe to assume all Christians know what the Bible says about race and ethnicity. Even Christians who have had the privilege of attending graduate school or seminary encounter few discussions of race and ethnicity from a Christian perspective, and the ones who do may have had a very general conversation about "equality" but little understanding in how to apply biblical teachings on racial justice. So a great place to start in the fight against racism is to teach what the Bible has to say on the topic. Here are some guidelines for doing so:

- *Give plenty of lead-up time for whatever course of study you decide to use.*
- *Remember to focus on community building and trust.*
- *Lay out what you've studied.*

What else stood out to you about this racial justice practice from Jemar's teaching in the video and from this chapter in *How to Fight Racism*?

_____
_____
_____
_____
_____
_____
_____
_____
_____
_____
_____

How will you put this practice into action in your own life?

_____

_____

_____

_____

_____

2. Learn Theology from the Disinherited

Any reformation in the way people think about race and ethnicity from a Christian perspective must include learning from people who have experienced marginalization and oppression. The presumed theological and intellectual superiority of European and white sources is itself an example of white supremacy and should be confronted whenever you teach about biblical ideas of race and ethnicity. Theologies developed by people of color should not receive any more or less scrutiny than those devised by European and white people. In fact, theologies developed by people of color provide a helpful context from the perspective of the poor and the politically oppressed as they looked to their faith to both explain and change their circumstances.

What else stood out to you about this racial justice practice from Jemar's teaching in the video and from this chapter in _How to Fight Racism_?

_____

_____

_____

_____

_____

_____

_____

_____

How will you put this practice into action in your own life?

_____

_____

_____

_____

_____

3. Treat Racism as It Should Be Treated: Like a Sin

While few churches would argue against the idea that racism is a sin, most will not deal with it as such. Too often racism is treated like an unlikable personality trait—something unsavory but not sinful. But in order to truly raise awareness about the threat of racism, white Christians should be prepared to bring charges against those who practice racism in word and deed. Churches should also educate their congregation about race and ethnicity from a biblical perspective and the idea of how applying the biblical teaching of the image of God is crucial for the journey toward racial justice.

What else stood out to you about this racial justice practice from Jemar's teaching in the video and from this chapter in *How to Fight Racism*?

_____
_____
_____
_____
_____
_____
_____

How will you put this practice into action in your own life?

_____
_____
_____
_____

Be Specific: Your Next Step

What specific step will you take this week as a result of what you've learned and explored today? Pay attention to the areas where you felt most convicted as you moved through this material. Perhaps there's a specific next step you need to take to lean into the areas of conviction or sensitivity you experienced today. Then give yourself a specific due date for your next step. Take it one step further and share your action step and your due date with a friend or colleague. It helps to have accountability in taking the next step.

Consider this: If you're struggling to think of something on your own, *consider the following biblical model for discipline to confront racism in your home, church, organization, or community.*

Read Matthew 18:15–20

If someone has committed a sin such as racism or racist acts against you or someone in your care, you can:

1. *Address the offender one-on-one—ideally this comes from the one who was offended.*
2. *If they refuse to admit their fault, then lovingly confront the person with an additional witness or two.*
3. *If the offender still refuses to listen, then take the matter to the leadership of your congregation or the organization.*
4. *If the offender continues in their denial, then they are to be treated as someone hostile to the faith or to the community; in this case, boundaries are required so no further harm can be done until the offender is willing to confess their wrong.*

As a result of what I learned in this session, I will:

_____

_____

_____

_____

_____

_____

_____

And I will do this by:
_____ (date)

Pray

Take a few moments to reflect on what you've learned today and over the course of session 2. Invite God into your racial justice journey. Ask God to show you areas in your life where you need to confess the ways you've treated others by denying them as image bearers of God. Thank God for his love, grace, and forgiveness for you and for all of humanity. Use this space to write out your prayer or journal your thoughts.

_____

_____

_____

_____

_____

_____

_____

For Next Week: Read chapter 3 in *How to Fight Racism* and use the space below to write any insights or questions from your personal study that you want to discuss at the next group meeting.

_____

_____

_____

_____

_____

_____

_____

_____

Journal, Reflections, and Notes

_____

_____

_____

_____

_____

_____

_____

_____

_____

_____

_____

_____

HOW TO EXPLORE YOUR RACIAL IDENTITY

*How can we come to grips with racism in
our own society if we don't come to grips
with racism in our own families?*
—JOAN DIDION

Welcome

Welcome to session 3 of *How to Fight Racism*. At some point in life, most
people have an encounter with racism that disrupts their previous thinking. These disruptive events sometimes jolt Black people and other people
of color into a new recognition of the salience of race in their own lives and
the broader culture. Throughout history people of color have had to endure
racial awakenings that destabilized their foundational beliefs about faith,
society, self, and others. Even white people who grew up in the age of "colorblindness" have to wake up to the relevance of race. The lens of colorblindness denies the historic and tangible ways that race affects people of
color and shapes the thinking and behaviors of white people. If the white
person chooses to journey toward racial awareness, then colorblindness
eventually gives way to color-consciousness. For people of all races, there
is a crucial need to critically explore their racial identity—a sense of their
own race—and ensure they are moving in a direction toward greater self-
awareness and sensitivity. This critical exploration is called *racial identity
development*, and it refers to the process of defining for oneself the personal
significance and social meaning of belonging to a particular racial group.
The word *development* indicates a process of change, which means that

racial identity is not static. One of the most valuable aspects of learning this racial-ethnic-cultural identity model is that it gives a framework for different stages of racial awareness. Knowing where you are in the stages of racial identity development can help you name the emotions you are feeling and can move you toward more mature levels of racial awareness. For every racial and ethnic group, individuals should be striving to recognize the ongoing importance of race in society today. Someone productively engaged in their own racial identity development will always be aware that they are more than the color of their skin—they are sons, daughters, spouses, workers, and believers. Racially mature people will assert not only that their race is a factor in how they experience the world but also that identity is more than skin deep. Let's take a closer look at growing in awareness on the journey toward racial justice.

Share

Take a few minutes to discuss one of the following statements:

- Share *one action or understanding* that has contributed to significant growth and development in your life as a Christian or as a person of faith.
  —or—
- What does it mean to explore your racial identity?

Watch

Play the video segment for session 3. As you watch, use the following outline to record any thoughts or concepts that stand out to you.

Notes
Teboho and the "Fees Must Fall" Movement in South Africa (2019)

Essential Understandings
Racial Identity Development
   Why Are All the Black Kids Sitting Together in the Cafeteria? by Beverly Daniel Tatum (2017).

Racial Justice Practices

1. Locate Where You Are in the Racial/Cultural Identity Development Chart

This will help you:

- provide vocabulary for your appropriate stage
- put words to your level of racial awakening or "wokeness"
- acknowledge your current stage of racial identity

The story of Daniel Hill.

The erroneous concept of "reverse" racism.

- race is a system of power and advantage
- prejudice + power

The Stats:

In Business	
2018	• 40 percent of people in America identified as racial or ethnic minorities
2019	• 4 percent of CEOs of Fortune 500 companies were Black • 11 percent were Latinos • 16 percent of boards of directors were racial or ethnic minorities
In Politics	
2018	• Sharese Davids (KS) and Deborah Pallend (NM) became the first two Native American women elected to the US House of Representatives
2013	• Tim Scott (SC) became the first African American from the South to serve in the US Senate

Race is not your own identity. . . . What racial identity development helps us to do, though, is have a healthy understanding of our racial, ethnic, and cultural background for ourselves and also for how we relate to other people.

—JEMAR TISBY

2. Explore Your Racial Autobiography

The slave narrative, a genre of literature, created:

- necessary agitation
- greater awareness of race

We have to come to terms with our own racial story.
Write it down. Writing prompts to follow:

- *What is your earliest memory of race?*
- *Have I had any negative experiences associated with my racial identity or that of someone else?*
- *When did I start growing racially conscious—when was my moment or series of awakening?*
- *From whom or in what period of life did I learn the most about my racial identity?*

> *I think we are well-advised to keep on nodding terms with the people we used to be, whether we find them attractive company or not.*
> —JOAN DIDION

3. Exploring Your Family's Racial Identity

Who we are as individuals is formed and shaped by our whole family (family systems therapy).

Exploring your family's racial identity is important:
- for your own development
- for confronting a past that may need confronting

> *How can we come to grips with racism in our own society if we don't come to grips with racism in our own families?*
> —JOAN DIDION

The best way to explore your family's racial identity: *Be honest about your purpose.*

4. Teach Your Kids about Race

How to do this:
- Educate yourself first.
- Push through your fears.
- Do it early; do it often.
- Don't just tell them; show them too.

Use the ARC of Racial Justice and these helpful reflective questions:

- *How do you build awareness for your kids about race and ethnicity?*
- *How do you help them intentionally build relationships across racial and ethnic lines?*
- *How can you show them that race operates according to systems, policies, and procedures and show them ways that they can be a force to fight against racism?*

The only wrong conversation to have with your kids about race is the one you don't have at all.
—JEMAR TISBY

5. Create a Pipeline of Black Mental Health Therapists and Other Therapists of Color

Racial and ethnic minorities represent 40% of the population, but 83.6% of mental health professionals identify as non-Hispanic White.
—PSYCHOLOGY TODAY

This means there is a gap in relating to people of color in:
- the experience of racism
- training of culturally aware practices

We can create this pipeline by providing:
- scholarships for people of color to go to school to become therapists
- support organizations providing mentorship, financial support, and encouragement

We have to be reflective about our own racial experiences in order to journey further down the road of racial justice.

Discuss

Take a few minutes with your group members to discuss what you just watched and explore these concepts in Scripture.

1. What stood out to you from Jemar's teaching on how to explore your racial identity?

   _____

   _____

   _____

   _____

2. Take an honest assessment. Locate the stage where you find yourself on the racial/cultural identity development chart. How did you get to this stage? What keeps you here?

   _____

   _____

   _____

   _____

3. How do you engage with others who talk about "reverse" racism?

   _____

   _____

   _____

   _____

4. You will have an opportunity to explore your racial autobiography after this session in your personal study time, but for the sake of learning in community as a group, let's answer a few of Jemar's questions together. What is your earliest memory of race?

   _____

   _____

   _____

   _____

5. Have you had any negative experiences associated with your own racial identity or that of someone else?

   _____

   _____

   _____

   _____

6. When did you start growing racially conscious? Was it a particular moment or series of moments that led to your awakening?

_____

_____

_____

7. What did you learn from your family of origin or your caregivers about racial identity? How did this shape your perspective?

_____

_____

_____

8. How do we build awareness about racial identity for our "kids" (the next generation) and help them build intentional relationships across racial and ethnic lines?

_____

_____

_____

Pray

Pray as a group before you close your time together. Ask God to show you where you are on the chart of racial/cultural identity development and where you need to grow. Use this space to keep track of prayer requests and group updates.

_____

_____

_____

_____

_____

_____

_____

_____

_____

_____

_____

BETWEEN-SESSIONS PERSONAL STUDY

Weekly Reflection

Before you begin the between-sessions exercises, briefly review your video notes for session 3. In the space below, write down the *most significant point* you took away from this session.

_____

_____

_____

_____

Diving Deeper: Essential Understandings

Reflect on the essential understandings Jemar provided in the video teaching, as well as the additional content for each of these essential understandings found in chapter 3 of *How to Fight Racism*. You may want to review the notes you took during the teaching session regarding each essential understanding as you read the corresponding questions.

1. Racial Identity Development

People often struggle to name what they are going through as they develop a greater sense of racial awareness. But social psychologists have a name for what it means to discover one's sense of race: *racial identity development*. This means each of us has constructed or is constructing ideas about what it means to be a white person or a person of color in a race-conscious society. And the stages of racial identity development range from unawareness, typically at younger ages or stages of maturity, to greater awareness as people get older and have more interactions with others.

What else stood out to you about this essential understanding from Jemar's teaching in the video and from this chapter in *How to Fight Racism*?

_____

_____

_____

_____

_____

_____

_____

How does this understanding change your view of the world around you?

_____

_____

_____

_____

Taking Action: Racial Justice Practices

Reflect on the racial justice practices Jemar provided in the video teaching, as well as the additional content for each of these practices found in chapter 3 of *How to Fight Racism*. You may want to review the notes you took during the teaching session regarding each racial justice practice as you read the corresponding questions.

1. Locate Where You Are in Your Racial/Cultural Identity Development

Knowing where you are in your racial identity development can help you name your emotions and can move you toward more mature levels of racial awareness. Taking a long hard look at your racial identity development requires a reassessment of your previous racial paradigms and begins a process of exploring your own racial and ethnic group with more intentionality. It also requires accepting and assuming responsibility to be a part of the solution.

What else stood out to you about this racial justice practice from Jemar's teaching in the video and from this chapter in *How to Fight Racism*?

_____

_____

_____

_____

_____

_____

_____

_____

How will you put this practice into action in your own life?

_____

_____

_____

_____

2. Write Your Racial Autobiography

One reason people struggle to talk productively about race is because they have not examined their own stories. And a lack of awareness around your own racial narrative will make it harder to locate your own racial identity development. For centuries, Black people have told stories of oppression and their pursuit of racial justice in a genre of literature known as the "slave narrative." In a similar way, recounting your story of race, whether as a member of a marginalized group or as a white person, can also create the kind of positive agitation needed for substantive change. A racial autobiography is a self-reported account of your history with race, and it will help you better understand your story—including your formative experiences around race—and build empathy for others. Use the following prompts to get started with your racial autobiography:

- *What is my earliest memory of race?*
- *Have I had any negative experiences associated with my racial identity or that of someone else?*
- *When did I start growing racially conscious—when was my awakening?*
- *From whom or in what period of life did I learn the most about my racial identity?*

- *Can I describe the different stages of racial identity development I've gone through and what made me aware of each?*
- *What concerns me about my racial past?*
- *What encourages me about my racial past?*
- *Why do I "do" racial justice? What is its purpose for me?*

_____

_____

_____

_____

_____

_____

_____

_____

_____

_____

_____

_____

_____

_____

_____

_____

_____

_____

_____

_____

What else stood out to you about this racial justice practice from Jemar's teaching in the video and from this chapter in *How to Fight Racism*?

_____

_____

_____

_____

_____

_____

How will you continue with this practice in your own life?

_____
_____
_____
_____
_____
_____
_____
_____
_____

3. Explore Your Family's Racial Identity

Exploring your racial identity would be incomplete without also delving into your family's past and present views and experiences with race. Much of who we are as individuals is shaped in community, especially by our families. To explore your family's racial identity, you will need to do some research and have some honest conversations. You will also need to prepare yourselves spiritually and emotionally for what you might find. You may feel shocked, saddened, and angered by your family's racial narrative, and you may also be encouraged. Perhaps you will even find helpful patterns in your life and experiences that you can use to teach your family members about what it looks like to consciously apply these helpful patterns in interactions with different people. Here are a few tips for getting started with your family's racial narrative:

- _Look at old family photos and try to identify who is in each picture. Do you know where they lived and in what era? Did they immigrate to the country? From where?_
- _Talk to siblings about race or racist attitudes in your family. They may remember incidents or feelings you do not._
- _Consult parents, grandparents, and other relatives about race or racist attitudes. Ask open-ended questions such as, "What was it like growing up in your family?" or "What do you remember about what was happening in your town when you were a teenager?"_
- _Be prepared for reluctance and resistance, and be honest about your purpose for inquiring: to better understand your racial history and identity._
- _Listen to their answers without offering judgment or analysis._

- *Take notes or record conversations if permission is granted by your family member.*

_____
_____
_____
_____
_____
_____
_____
_____
_____
_____
_____
_____
_____
_____
_____
_____
_____
_____
_____
_____
_____
_____
_____

What else stood out to you about this racial justice practice from Jemar's teaching in the video and from this chapter in *How to Fight Racism*?

_____
_____
_____
_____
_____
_____
_____
_____

How will you put this practice into action in your own life?

_____

_____

_____

_____

4. Teach Your Kids about Race

The stakes are high as we train our children to value everyone and treat people with dignity. You won't be able to adequately respond as an adult if you haven't already thought through how you might teach children about race. You've taken an important step on the journey by participating in this study. And the more you increase your capacity around issues of race and racism, the better you will be able to teach young people about the topic—whether they are your own children or the children in your consistent care. Learning what the Bible says about how to treat people who are different and exploring your racial autobiography are crucial elements that will help you respond in the right ways. Here are a few suggested practices for teaching your kids about race:

- _First, teach yourself._
- _Push through your fears and talk about them._
- _Make it an ongoing dialogue, not just a one-time conversation._
- _Use concrete examples and experiences—such as drawing pictures with a box of crayons with a full spectrum of colors or traveling to a place that has an important story to tell about racial justice or injustice._
- _Use the culture, spaces, and relationships kids encounter every day._

What else stood out to you about this racial justice practice from Jemar's teaching in the video and from this chapter in _How to Fight Racism_?

_____

_____

_____

_____

_____

_____

_____

_____

How will you put these practices into action with your own kids or with children who are in your care at times?

_____

_____

_____

_____

5. Create a Pipeline of Black Mental Health Therapists

Racial trauma is contextual and specific. It derives from particular characteristics and social experiences connected to social meanings that one's race or ethnicities carry. These wounds are so particular that it can be hard for a white person to understand and effectively treat clients of color who have mental health issues related to their experience of racism. And then there is the challenge of preparing therapists to serve a diverse racial and ethnic clientele, and this affects their training and curriculum. The scarcity of therapists from racial and ethnic minority groups, often due to economic access of the required graduate degrees, along with a lag in culturally responsive training materials, means there is an urgent need to diversify both the demographics and curricula of the mental health profession.

What else stood out to you about this racial justice practice from Jemar's teaching in the video and from this chapter in *How to Fight Racism*?

_____

_____

_____

_____

_____

_____

_____

_____

How will you put this practice into action in your own life?

_____

_____

_____

_____

Be Specific: Your Next Step

What specific step will you take this week as a result of what you've learned and explored today? Pay attention to the areas where you felt most convicted as you moved through this material.

Consider this: If you're struggling to think of something on your own, *follow the prompts to write your own racial autobiography, and then take it one step further to explore your family's racial identity too.*

As a result of what I learned in this session, I will:

_____

_____

_____

_____

_____

_____

And I will do this by:

_____ (date)

Pray

Take a few moments to reflect on what you've learned today and over the course of session 3. Invite God into your racial justice journey. Ask God to give you the courage to take a hard, honest look at your racial identity development and the racial identity of your family system. Thank God for his grace and forgiveness, and his willingness to help you be more intentional about your personal journey toward racial justice, no matter what happened in generations past. Use this space to write out your prayer or journal your thoughts.

_____

_____

_____

_____

_____

_____

For Next Week: Read chapter 4 in *How to Fight Racism* and use the space below to write any insights or questions from your personal study that you want to discuss at the next group meeting.

_____
_____
_____
_____
_____
_____
_____

Journal, Reflections, and Notes

_____
_____
_____
_____
_____
_____
_____
_____
_____
_____
_____
_____
_____
_____
_____
_____
_____
_____
_____

HOW TO STUDY THE HISTORY OF RACE

The past is never dead. It's not even past.
—WILLIAM FAULKNER

Welcome

Welcome to session 4 of *How to Fight Racism*. History does not, in fact, repeat itself. But history does rhyme. We can hear cadences and syncopations of the past in the present. And learning about history is more than learning about what happened before; it is about understanding what is happening now. In order to effectively fight racism, we must learn from the past. And we must develop a greater awareness of race as it has played out in our communities, nation, and world. Learning about the history of race is a task for everyone, no matter your race or ethnicity. Rightly remembering communal stories is a way of situating ourselves within the broader narrative. History tells us who and where we come from, how the people and events before us have shaped who we are now, and what kind of actions we need to take to pursue a more racially just future. We also must understand that there is no objectivity in history. All historical treatments hold some sort of bias. This is not necessarily a bad thing as long as you know history-telling has an element of subjectivity. If all history has some sort of slant and is subject factual error, this understanding begs for the question, *how do we know which history to trust?* The purpose of this session is to develop an awareness about trustworthy history as it relates to race. And it will give us the historical context necessary for identifying and fighting racism in the present day. The ARC of Racial Justice reminds us that building our awareness necessarily includes learning more about the history of racism. As we explore the causes and consequences of racism, history provides the vital context of the past to pursue solutions in the present that are rooted in a firm understanding of racial justice.

Share

Take a few minutes to discuss one of the following statements:

- Share one important piece you've explored regarding the history of race.

  —*or*—

- How have you studied the history of race before? Briefly share why, how, and when.

Watch

Play the video segment for session 4. As you watch, use the following outline to record any thoughts or concepts that stand out to you.

Notes

> *For history, as nearly no one seems to know, is not merely something to be read, and it does not refer merely or principally to the past. On the contrary, the great force of history comes from the fact that we carry it within us. Are unconsciously controlled by it. And history is literally present in all that we do.*
>
> **—JAMES BALDWIN, "UNNAMEABLE OBJECTS, UNSPEAKABLE CRIMES" (1966)**

The History of Race

> *In order to effectively fight racism, we have to know how the past influences the present.*
>
> **—JEMAR TISBY**

History does not repeat itself, but it does rhyme.

Essential Understandings
Why History Is Important

1. HISTORY IS CONTEXT

> *If we want to understand the world around us,*
> *then we have to understand what happened*
> *before—what led us to this point.*
> **—JEMAR TISBY**

Mike Brown, Ferguson, MO (2014)

2. HISTORY IS ABOUT IDENTITY

Learning the stories of the people who came before us and how these stories shaped us

3. *AD FONTES*—BACK TO THE SOURCES

> *150 years after the civil war began, 48% percent of*
> *respondents thought the Civil War was about States' rights,*
> *compared to 38% who thought it was about slavery.*
> **—PEW RESEARCH SURVEY (2011)**

"Articles of Succession"
Alexander Stephens, VP of the Confederacy (1861)

Racial Justice Practices
1. Learn from Trustworthy Historical Resources

> *But the idea of an objective version of history-telling,*
> *from which all others are deviant, is an absurdity.*
> *There is no objectivity in History. The very act of*
> *selecting a topic, for example, is privileging certain*
> *facts—making them "historical"—over others.*
> **—KEVIN GANNON**

- Go back to the primary source(s) and fact check.
- Beware of Whiggish interpretations of history.

2. Take Down Confederate Monuments and Symbols

> *These monuments purposefully celebrate a fictional,*
> *sanitized Confederacy; ignoring the death, ignoring the*
> *enslavement, and the terror that it actually stood for.*
> —MITCH LANDRIEU, FORMER MAYOR OF NEW ORLEANS

Objections:
- "This erases history"—however, there is a big difference between veneration and remembrance.
- "It's about heritage, not hate"—however, the heritage of the Confederacy *is* hate.

3. Commemorate Juneteenth

June 1865—the day enslaved Black people finally learned the Civil War had been won and emancipation was on its way

- It forces us to look back—to reflect and lament.

> *Juneteenth . . . forces us to look backward and*
> *see where we've been, particularly to reckon with*
> *the fact that this nation's wealth was built upon*
> *the enslavement of people of African descent.*
> —JEMAR TISBY

- It causes us to celebrate.
- It reminds us how far we still have to go.

What more must we do?

Other Racial Justice Practices Include:
- Learn from academic historians.
- Do research on your local community.
- Do an oral history of people you know or people involved in momentous events in racial justice history.

> *The past is never dead. It's not even past.*
> —WILLIAM FAULKNER

History provides the context for unlocking the present.

Discuss

Take a few minutes with your group members to discuss what you just watched and explore these concepts in Scripture.

1. What stood out to you from Jemar's teaching on how to study the history of race?

   _____

   _____

   _____

2. According to Jemar, why is understanding history so important when it comes to fighting racial injustice?

   _____

   _____

   _____

3. How does the history of race influence our understanding and experience of racism today?

   _____

   _____

   _____

4. Which of these suggested racial justice practices have you already participated in, and why?

   _____

   _____

   _____

5. What do you say to the critics of these practices? Share a personal experience, if you have any, from participating in these practices.

   _____

   _____

   _____

6. How are you being mindful to learn from trustworthy historical resources?

_____

_____

_____

7. Are there any Confederate monuments or symbols being used in the places and spaces where you live, work, worship, and play? If so, do you plan to play a part in having these monuments and symbols removed?

_____

_____

_____

8. How will you plan to commemorate Juneteenth as an individual and as a community? Consider what it must be like for your friends of color to watch you celebrate July 4 but not Juneteenth. Ask them how you can join in their celebration.

_____

_____

_____

Pray

Pray as a group before you close your time together. Ask God to give you wisdom and perspective to see how important understanding history is to the journey toward racial justice. Use this space to keep track of prayer requests and group updates.

_____

_____

_____

_____

_____

_____

_____

_____

_____

BETWEEN-SESSIONS PERSONAL STUDY

Weekly Reflection

Before you begin the between-sessions exercises, briefly review your video notes for session 4. In the space below, write down the *most significant point* you took away from this session.

_____

_____

_____

_____

_____

_____

Diving Deeper: Essential Understandings

Reflect on the essential understandings Jemar provided in the video teaching, as well as the additional content for each of these essential understandings found in chapter 4 of *How to Fight Racism*. You may want to review the notes you took during the teaching session regarding each essential understanding as you read the corresponding questions.

1. Study History

If you want to understand the present, you must first understand the past. And to learn history is to learn context. Most good seminary professors and pastors teach that in order to read the Bible effectively, you must know the context of the part of the Bible you are reading. It is like the men of Issachar in the Bible who "understood the times" (1 Chron. 12:32). We need to study history not simply to know more about the past but also to know more about ourselves. History is about identity. Without a sense of history, we lose our sense of self.

What else stood out to you about this essential understanding from Jemar's teaching in the video and from this chapter in *How to Fight Racism*?

_____

_____

_____

_____

_____

_____

_____

_____

_____

_____

_____

_____

How does this understanding change your view of the world around you?

_____

_____

_____

_____

2. *Ad Fontes*

This is the rallying cry of the Protestant Reformation of the sixteenth century. *Ad fontes* is a Latin phrase that means *back to the sources* because having an emphasis on primary sources is a key tenant of doing good history. And learning about the history of race has transformative power because it shows not simply what people believed or aspired to but also what they actually did. And it is the factual basis of history that makes it so effective in understanding race.

What else stood out to you about this essential understanding from Jemar's teaching in the video and from this chapter in *How to Fight Racism*?

_____
_____
_____
_____
_____
_____
_____

How does this understanding change your view of the world around you?

_____
_____
_____
_____
_____

Taking Action: Racial Justice Practices

Now reflect on the racial justice practices Jemar provided in the video teaching, as well as the additional content for each of these practices found in chapter 4 of *How to Fight Racism*. You may want to review the notes you took during the teaching session regarding each racial justice practice as you read the corresponding questions.

1. Learn from Academic Historians

Academic historians have dedicated their careers to the careful study of the past. They have spent incalculable hours in the stacks at libraries pouring over thousands of documents in the archives and in lonely offices pondering how to make sense of the past. They have also subjected their work to peer review by having other experts in the field examine their research to offer critique and correction, which results in the collaborative effort of professional standards required by academic discipline. And the work of academic historians is typically more detailed and well-attested information compared to that of popular history books found on the shelves at large chain bookstores. To learn from academic historians, follow these two helpful tips:

- *Determine your areas of interest. What time period do you want to learn about? What nation or community? What aspect of history— gender, race, politics, culture?*
- *Look for books from university presses. They focus on publishing texts from scholars whose work has undergone rigorous preparation and revision.*

What else stood out to you about this racial justice practice from Jemar's teaching in the video and from this chapter in *How to Fight Racism*?

_____
_____
_____
_____
_____
_____
_____
_____
_____

How will you put this practice into action in your own life?

_____
_____
_____
_____

2. Find Trustworthy History

History is a combination of an assemblage of the facts, interpretation, and opinion based on what topics people choose, what questions they ask, what access they have to resources, how they arrange the facts, and what meaning they give to historical events. And at the end of the day, this all depends on subjective reasoning. This leaves many of us wondering: How do we know which history to trust? Because history always has some sort of slant and is subject to factual error, we must search for histories that honor the complexity of the human experience. Here are a few suggestions on how to find trustworthy history:

- *Seek out primary sources. This is the best way to verify the facts and decide for yourself what they mean.*

- *Rely on multiple sources for historical data. This is the best way to cross check information to see if there's a consensus.*
- *Be wary of any history that casts the story of humanity as one of inevitable progress with clear heroes and villains. This type of narrative usually obscures more than it reveals.*

What else stood out to you about this racial justice practice from Jemar's teaching in the video and from this chapter in *How to Fight Racism*?

_____

_____

_____

_____

_____

_____

_____

_____

How will you continue with this practice in your own life?

_____

_____

_____

_____

3. Learn Your Local History

Important history is all around us, but the significance of what happened nearby can sometimes be lost because familiarity leads to invisibility. Sometimes we grow so accustomed to seeing our surroundings that we have to rediscover how to interrogate our environment to glean lessons from the past. One of the best places to start learning about the history of race is right where you are. Here are a few proactive steps you can take to learn about your local history:

- *Learn about the names that surround you—on street signs, buildings, counties, and cities. They explain part of your community's history and what the community values.*
- *Learn about the original inhabitants of your community. Who were they and where are they now? Beyond simply knowing the name of the tribe, learn the history of that tribe or nation. What language did they speak?*

What treaties or wars led to their displacement? What is the state of the tribe in present day?

- *Find out who your state honors in the National Statuary Hall Collection.*
- *Take down Confederate monuments and symbols. Monuments and symbols are about memory, how we choose to remember the past. We need to remove all statues and symbols of racism and replace them with commemorations of those who fought for the dignity and equality of all people.*

What else stood out to you about this racial justice practice from Jemar's teaching in the video and from this chapter in *How to Fight Racism*?

_____
_____
_____
_____
_____
_____
_____
_____

How will you put this practice into action in your own life?

_____
_____
_____
_____

4. Conduct an Oral History

Before human beings created written language, they passed down stories of their families and communities through oral histories. Often poetry and song, and even role-playing, were a part of this oral history-telling. In doing so, these ancient people groups preserved the history and the heritage of their peoples. They are why oral history is known as *a method of gathering, preserving, and interpreting the voices and memories of people, communities, and participants in past events* (Oral History Association). We cannot prolong anyone's life indefinitely, but we can honor their stories by inviting them to recount and record these narratives. And the goal of doing so is to understand the historical context of a community through the lens of a particular person. Here are some tips for collecting oral history:

- *Clearly identify your purpose in collecting and sharing an oral history.*
- *Come to the conversation having already done your homework so you know what questions to ask.*
- *Send the questions ahead of time, if possible, so people have time to think and collect tangible artifacts.*

You can ask open-ended questions such as:

- *What was school like growing up?*
- *What was your first job?*
- *Can you describe the racial climate where you grew up?*
- *Did you grow up in a religious community? What did the people around you communicate about race?*
- *Do any incidents around race stand out to you?*

What else stood out to you about this racial justice practice from Jemar's teaching in the video and from this chapter in *How to Fight Racism*?

_____
_____
_____
_____
_____
_____
_____
_____

How will you put this practice into action in your own life?

_____
_____
_____
_____

5. Conduct an Institutional History

Organizations, churches, denominations, and other religious institutions can also examine their organizational histories to understand the context of a community through the lens of an institution. This is important work for organizations that are serious about racial justice. Remembrance and repair begin at home—meaning all communities and organizations need to explore their ties to racism and white supremacy in order to have the integrity necessary to speak about racial justice today. Organizations that conduct institutional history start to "unearth and understand" their racial past and move forward on the journey of transformation toward racial justice.

What else stood out to you about this racial justice practice from Jemar's teaching in the video and from this chapter in *How to Fight Racism*?

_____

_____

_____

_____

_____

_____

How will you put this practice into action in your own life?

_____

_____

_____

_____

6. Commemorate Juneteenth

Juneteenth is what's called a "portmanteau" consisting of two words, *June* and *nineteenth*, and it stands as the oldest celebration of Black emancipation in the United States. It comes from June 19, 1865—the day news finally reached the enslaved Black people in Texas that the Civil War had ended and their emancipation was on its way. In the wake of the announcement, which came a full two years after the Emancipation Proclamation and a full two months after Robert E. Lee surrendered to Ulysses S. Grant, Black people erupted into celebration. They were now at the dawn of freedom. Historically speaking, few events compare to the significance of the abolition of slavery in the United States. Yet our nation does relatively little to reflect its importance. Here's why it's important to remember, commemorate, and celebrate Juneteenth today:

- *It reminds Americans that their country was birthed with racist ideology.*
- *It is an opportunity to celebrate progress.*
- *It reminds us of the work that still needs to be done.*

And here is how churches can celebrate Juneteenth as a racial justice practice:

- *Read a statement of commemoration during services.*
- *Preach a sermon or record a special message on liberation.*
- *Host a Sunday school class or Bible study on history and liberation.*
- *Bring in guest speakers (historians, preachers, community leaders, etc.).*
- *Host a picnic or festival for the public.*
- *Offer a financial donation to a Black-led organization or a museum dedicated to Black history.*

And if you are white, consider celebrating Juneteenth by:

- *Rejoicing along with Black people while remembering the white supremacy your ancestors created and from which you still benefit.*
- *Support Black churches or organizations as they celebrate Juneteenth.*
- *Host a teach-in for other white people to learn about slavery and its legacies.*
- *Use it as a day to advocate for political and systemic changes that lead to racial justice.*

What else stood out to you about this racial justice practice from Jemar's teaching in the video and from this chapter in *How to Fight Racism*?

_____
_____
_____
_____
_____
_____
_____
_____

How will you continue with this practice in your own life?

_____
_____
_____
_____
_____

Be Specific: Your Next Step

What specific step will you take this week as a result of what you've learned and explored today? Pay attention to the areas where you felt most convicted as you moved through this material.

Consider this: If you're struggling to think of something, *consider how you might help your church community or local congregation celebrate Juneteenth by practicing one of the recommended suggestions.*

As a result of what I learned in this session, I will:

_____
_____
_____
_____
_____
_____

And I will do this by:
_____ (date)

Pray

Take a few moments to reflect on what you've learned today and over the course of session 4. Invite God into the awareness needed for your racial justice journey today. Ask God to show you how and where to take next steps to study the history of race. Ask God for a friend or mentor who will provide perspective and study alongside you. Thank God for the important context of history as we understand the past and make sense of the present. Use this space to write out your prayer or journal your thoughts.

_____
_____
_____
_____
_____

For Next Week: Read chapter 5 in *How to Fight Racism* and use the space below to write any insights or questions from your personal study that you want to discuss at the next group meeting.

_____

_____

_____

_____

_____

_____

_____

_____

_____

_____

Journal, Reflections, and Notes

_____

_____

_____

_____

_____

_____

_____

_____

_____

_____

_____

_____

_____

_____

_____

_____

_____

_____

HOW TO DO RECONCILIATION RIGHT

The Word became flesh and made his dwelling among us.

—JOHN 1:14

Welcome

Welcome to session 5 of *How to Fight Racism*. The power of reconciliation holds true across times, places, and cultures. It transcends our natural tendencies toward self-centeredness in relationships and leads us to new heights of understanding others. But reconciliation with other people is not simply a matter of strategy, practices, and logical choices—it is a *spiritual* matter too. For those who do not consider themselves religious, one does not have to adhere to any particular religion to acknowledge the moral imperatives of reconciliation. Reconciling people across racial and ethnic boundaries reduces friction between groups, opens channels of communication and understanding, and moves communities toward inclusivity. That's why the topic of reconciliation is so important to understanding the ARC of Racial Justice. *Reconciliation is core to our relationships.* And reconciliation is connected deeply to our faith because we need a transcendent framework to guide us on the journey toward racial justice, love, and wholeness. Reconciliation is one of the key tools in understanding the spiritual dimensions of race relations in the fight against racism. Understanding the problems of racial ruptures at a spiritual level can aid attempts to bring healing through reconciliation. And this understanding comes from the demonstrated truth that all reconciliation is relational: the Son of God becoming human in Jesus Christ. This is known as the incarnation, when God took on a human body ultimately to reconcile us to himself—to repair the rupture in the relationship between God and humanity that occurred in the garden of Eden. This is the ultimate example and the ultimate sacrifice of reconciliation. This is where we get the divine morality that compels us to build or restore relationships with one another. And this is not just for individuals. Communities and churches can work to bring about reconciliation in relationships too.

Share

Take a few minutes to discuss one of the following statements:

- Share one word or phrase you would use to describe what it's like to have a rupture in your close relationships.
    —or—
- What does reconciliation mean to you?

Watch

Play the video segment for session 5. As you watch, use the following outline to record any thoughts or concepts that stand out to you.

Notes
The ARC of Racial Justice
- Awareness
- **Relationships**
- Commitment

The "talk" Black parents have to have with their kids

Reconciliation

Essential Understandings
1. All Reconciliation Is Relational
- Reconciled to God through the birth and death of Jesus
- Reconciled to each other

We can never neglect the importance
of relationships in pursuing
reconciliation and racial justice.
—JEMAR TISBY

2. Reconciliation
- There was a time when all things were at peace (Gen. 1–2).
- Reconciliation refers to a pattern—not a time period—of harmony, love, and mutual respect as set by God.
- We have the ministry of reconciliation—the Biblical concept and our responsibility to be reconciled to one another.

3. There Is a "Right" Way to Do Racial Reconciliation
- 1995—the Southern Baptist Convention repented of its proslavery origins
- 1996—the Promise Keepers movement held a rally that set out to "Break Down the Walls"

For he himself [Jesus Christ] is our peace, who
has made the two groups one and has destroyed
the barrier, the dividing wall of hostility.
—EPHESIANS 2:14

- 2012—the SBC elected its first Black president, Fred Leuter

Problems
There are some problems with modern racial reconciliation movements:

A. A *misdiagnosis* of the problem: the problem is separation, and desegregation is the solution.
B. The notion of power dynamics within relationships is excluded. Diversity and desegregation are two separate things.

What we have to do is move toward equity
where everyone has a seat at the table, but they
also have a voice at the table too, where their
opinions and their perspective matter.
—JEMAR TISBY

C. The issue of gender is neglected or downplayed.

> *Women, particularly women of color, have largely*
> *been invisible in the field of reconciliation.*
> —CHANEQUA WALKER-BARNES, *I BRING*
> *THE VOICES OF MY PEOPLE* (2019)

So how can we do racial reconciliation right?

Racial Justice Practices

1. Incorporate Lamentation into Worship

> *Putting words to your pain helps you process that pain.*
> —JEMAR TISBY

The Bible:
- Lamentations
- Psalms

> *When it comes to racial justice, one of the things that we need*
> *to do in order to do reconciliation right is lament how we've*
> *done reconciliation wrong for so long and in so many ways.*
> —JEMAR TISBY

How to lament:
- Pray specifically
- Confess

> *I am too ashamed and disgraced, my God, to lift up my*
> *face to you, because our sins are higher than our heads*
> *and our guilt has reached to the heavens. From the days*
> *of our ancestors until now, our guilt has been great.*
> —EZRA 9:6–7

> *Even though each person is responsible for their own actions,*
> *our sense of morality and our conscience is shaped by community.*
> —JEMAR TISBY

2. Do a History of Your Local Congregation

This is especially important if you belong to a predominantly white church that has existed since the 1980s or earlier.

3. Go Back and Be Reconciled with the People Who Have Been Harmed By Racism

- Acknowledge what you've done.
- Acknowledge what you've learned.
- *Then* acknowledge what you're going to do next or in the future.

4. Preach and Teach about Reconciliation

- From the pulpit
- In Sunday school
- In small groups

---

1. Where in this text do we find equality envisioned and represented by physical presence?
2. Where in this text do we notice empathy as a catalyst or bridge to create opportunities to overcome the past and make new decisions for justice and peace?
3. Where do we find wisdom and truth in this ancient text, the wisdom of the ages?
4. Where is the language of poetry and art that lifts and elevates by touching the emotive chords of wonder, hope, and mystery?

—FRANK A. THOMAS, *HOW TO PREACH A DANGEROUS SERMON* (2018)

Pay attention to:

- Justice
- Peace
- Reconciliation

There would be no black church without racism in the white church. The reality is, as churches, we must confess, lament, and repair the damage done by racism.

—JEMAR TISBY

Discuss

Take a few minutes with your group members to discuss what you just watched and explore these concepts in Scripture.

1. What stood out to you from Jemar's teaching on how to do reconciliation right?

   _____

   _____

   _____

2. According to Jemar, how has God set the relational framework for reconciliation throughout Scripture?

   _____

   _____

   _____

3. Do you actually think reconciliation is possible in today's world? Why or why not?

   _____

   _____

   _____

4. What positive experiences or healthy attempts at reconciliation have you witnessed lately? How have you recently participated in acts of reconciliation?

   _____

   _____

   _____

5. In his teaching, Jemar said, "Diversity and desegregation are two different things." What did he mean by this?

   _____

   _____

   _____

   _____

6. What does the practice of lament mean to you? How has it been incorporated or excluded from your spiritual practices?

_____

_____

_____

7. Which racial justice practice do you think would have the greatest impact on your faith community?

_____

_____

_____

8. How do you think your church would respond if you put all of the practices into action over the next few months? What could be the impact? What could be the roadblocks or hurdles?

_____

_____

_____

Pray

Pray as a group before you close your time together. Ask God to convict your church leaders and your community on where you need to confess, repent, and take action toward racial reconciliation _together_. Use this space to keep track of prayer requests and group updates.

_____

_____

_____

_____

_____

_____

_____

_____

_____

_____

_____

BETWEEN-SESSIONS PERSONAL STUDY

Weekly Reflection

Before you begin the between-sessions exercises, briefly review your video notes for session 5. In the space below, write down the *most significant point* you took away from this session.

_____

_____

_____

_____

Diving Deeper: Essential Understandings

Reflect on the essential understandings Jemar provided in the video teaching, as well as the additional content for each of these essential understandings found in chapter 5 of *How to Fight Racism*. You may want to review the notes you took during the teaching session regarding each essential understanding as you read the corresponding questions.

1. Racial Justice Often Begins with Relationships

Many times, people need personal motivation to disrupt the regular patterns of racism in their lives and in society. Often it is a relationship or friendship that changes a person's perspective. It is difficult to pursue effective structural remedies to racism if you have little understanding of the personal experiences of marginalized people. It's helpful if you read a book on the Civil Rights movement, but hearing grief in the voice of someone who lived through it will leave a more lasting impression. Relationships make reconciliation real and motivate us to act.

What else stood out to you about this essential understanding from Jemar's teaching in the video and from this chapter in *How to Fight Racism*?

_____
_____
_____
_____
_____
_____
_____
_____
_____
_____
_____
_____
_____

How does this understanding change your view of the world around you?

_____
_____
_____
_____
_____
_____

2. Conciliation or Reconciliation?

Given the tumultuous history of race relations, the concept of reconciliation can seem as realistic as taking a running leap from Earth and touching the moon. That is why some people will object to the very concept of reconciliation between different racial and ethnic groups. They ask, *when have we ever been at peace*, or *when have we ever had a healthy relationship that can be restored?* If different races of people have never had conciliation, how can they have reconciliation? If it is possible to speak of reconciliation with God going all the way back to the beginning of humanity when there was harmony, then it is also possible to speak of reconciliation between people of different racial and ethnic groups.

What else stood out to you about this essential understanding from Jemar's teaching in the video and from this chapter in *How to Fight Racism*?

_____

_____

_____

_____

_____

_____

_____

_____

_____

_____

_____

_____

_____

_____

How does this understanding change your view of the world around you?

_____

_____

_____

_____

_____

_____

3. The Problem with Reconciliation

The concept of racial reconciliation has been voided of its transformational power in many circles. In evangelical Christian circles, racial reconciliation—as it is practiced here—suffers from three main shortcomings: *it misdiagnoses the problem as separation, it does not properly address power dynamics*, and *it does not take gender into account*. The misdiagnosis of the problem is due to the fact that racism is often reduced to individual behaviors and attitudes in evangelical circles, and an individualistic understanding of reconciliation presents racial separation as the problem. Improperly addressing power dynamics means that there is still a lack in diversity in the leadership of most Christian organizations. And women—particularly women of color—are largely invisible in the field of racial reconciliation. Despite these problems, racial reconciliation is still a worthy goal if we can recover its true definition and do reconciliation the right way.

What else stood out to you about this essential understanding from Jemar's teaching in the video and from this chapter in *How to Fight Racism*?

_____

_____

_____

_____

_____

_____

_____

How does this understanding change your view of the world around you?

_____

_____

_____

_____

_____

Taking Action: Racial Justice Practices

Now reflect on the racial justice practices Jemar provided in the video teaching, as well as the additional content for each of these practices found in chapter 5 of *How to Fight Racism*. You may want to review the notes you took during the teaching session regarding each racial justice practice as you read the corresponding questions.

1. Incorporate Lamentation into Worship

When love is betrayed and people hurt others because of racial arrogance, it is cause for lament. And if you have not learned to lament, then you have not learned to love. Singing our sadness grants a measure of control amid chaos. If we can put words to our hurt, then we can, in some sense, deal with the harm on our own terms. When we express lament through song, it has a way of lifting the soul out of despair. This is why every community dedicated to racial justice should have a canon of songs devoted to lament. Lament should also be expressed in prayer. And public prayer practices of lament may include:

- *A reading of the names of people unjustly killed by law enforcement*
- *A litany of injustices perpetrated by the local, state, and federal governments we empower*
- *A confession of the community's failure to love and serve the poor, the prisoner, the widow, and the orphan*
- *A reading from Scripture that expresses lament: Exodus 34:8–9, Lamentations 1:17–22, Matthew 23:37–39, etc.*

What else stood out to you about this racial justice practice from Jemar's teaching in the video and from this chapter in *How to Fight Racism*?

_____

_____

_____

_____

_____

_____

_____

_____

_____

How does this understanding change your view of the world around you?

_____

_____

_____

_____

_____

2. Corporately Confess the Sin of Racism

Racial justice resisters will argue that no one can be expected to repent of racist acts they did not personally commit. But their argument fails based on what the Bible teaches about confession: *leaders must take responsibility for those they represent.* Biblical leaders like Ezra (Ezra 9:6–7) understood the communal nature of sin and righteousness. While each person within a community is responsible for his or her own choices, one's moral conscience is formed in relationship with a community of people. This means that all people in a community have a responsibility to examine the boundaries of their bigotry, and all bear the responsibility of communal confession of the sin of racism. We examine the boundaries of bigotry within our communities by asking:

- *What has our community tolerated when it comes to racism?*
- *What prejudice has it permitted?*
- *What has our community determined to be the acceptable pace of change?*

What else stood out to you about this racial justice practice from Jemar's teaching in the video and from this chapter in *How to Fight Racism*?

_____

_____

_____

_____

_____

_____

How will you put this practice into action in your own life?

_____

_____

_____

_____

_____

3. Acknowledge Your Church's Racial History

Any church, especially those that have been in existence for a long time, should engage in a process of uncovering and confessing their racial history. In exploring their racial histories, some churches find exclusion and overt racism, some find silence in times when racism ran amok in their communities, and some find cause for gratitude. Historically, white churches will almost always have an uneven record on race at best. But moments of courageous Christianity can be instructive and inspirational in our present-day fight against racism because only what is revealed can be healed. It does no service to a community to hide its shortcomings. Failures of racial justice must be faced with humility, truth, and courage. Here are a few tips for discovering your church's racial history:

- *Commission a historian to do the research, conduct the interviews, and write the story of your church—a respectful but unvarnished story.*
- *Implement a plan—once the data has been gathered—for church leaders to share the information with the congregation members.*
- *Call a special meeting to disseminate the findings and answer initial questions.*
- *Make a plan of action for the church to move away from its racist past and address any present-day obstacles to racial justice.*
- *Teach and preach the plan of action—in Sunday school, Bible study, weekend sermons—to make sure everyone in your church has an opportunity to hear the message and process the issues raised.*
- *Train facilitators who will be having these conversations, including the pastoral staff.*
- *Use role playing, outside consultation, coaching, and more to de-escalate tense situations and answer complex questions with wisdom and empathy.*
- *Make the story and the plan of action accessible to all—a church's record on race should not be hidden from visitors or potential members.*

What else stood out to you about this racial justice practice from Jemar's teaching in the video and from this chapter in *How to Fight Racism*?

_____

_____

_____

_____

_____

_____

_____

_____

_____

_____

How will you put this practice into action in your own life?

_____

_____

_____

_____

_____

4. Reconcile with People Harmed by Your Church through Racism

Even decades after hurtful experiences, Black people and other people of color find that the racism—especially when it happens in the church or among fellow Christians—lingers in their hearts and minds, and sometimes so does the anger. That's why a new generation of white Christians will have to go to great lengths to repair the damage. And even then, reconciliation does not always have tidy endings. But a church has not truly reckoned with its racism until it ceases to hide it. Perfection on race is not a requirement for progress, but honesty is. Here are a few tips for reconciliation within a church when people have been harmed by racism:

- *Reveal to the congregation the racist origins of the church and adopt the denominational stance on race and the gospel.*
- *Study what the Bible says about individual and corporate repentance.*
- *Publicly confess and repent of racism.*
- *Recommit to serving the local community across racial and ethnic lines.*

What else stood out to you about this racial justice practice from Jemar's teaching in the video and from this chapter in *How to Fight Racism*?

_____

_____

_____

_____

_____

_____

_____

_____

_____

_____

How will you put this practice into action in your own life?

_____

_____

_____

_____

_____

5. Preach about Racial Reconciliation

Milquetoast or feeble sermons about all people being equal in God's sight and injunctions to treat everyone fairly is like going for a swim and calling it a shower. You get wet, but you don't get clean. Pastors and other church leaders must know the particular contours of their congregation well enough to identify the racial idols of their people and then tear them down by calling out, confessing, and condemning racism. Confession requires naming specific sins. That's why leaders must cite specific beliefs or actions held by their community members and identify why they are racist. In the book *How to Preach a Dangerous Sermon*, Frank A. Thomas recommends asking these five questions in sermon preparation to spur the moral imagination for justice:

- *Where in this text do we find equality envisioned and represented by physical presence?*
- *Where in this text do we notice empathy as a catalyst or bridge to create opportunities to overcome the past and make new decisions for peace and justice?*
- *Where do we find wisdom and truth in this ancient text, the wisdom of the ages?*
- *Where is the language of poetry and art that lifts and elevates by touching the emotive chords of wonder, hope, and mystery?*
- *To what contemporary moral concern would you apply your responses in these four questions above?*

What else stood out to you about this racial justice practice from Jemar's teaching in the video and from this chapter in *How to Fight Racism*?

_____

_____

_____

_____

_____

_____

_____

_____

_____

_____

_____

How will you put this practice into action in your own life?

_____
_____
_____
_____
_____

Be Specific: Your Next Step

What specific step will you take this week as a result of what you've learned and explored today? Pay attention to the areas where you felt most convicted as you moved through this material.

Consider this: If you're struggling to think of something on your own, *consider how your church might talk about racism from the pulpit or in front of the camera,* or *how you might facilitate Bible study or have a conversation regarding Scripture and racism by answering the five questions posed by Frank A. Thomas.*

As a result of what I learned in this session, I will:

_____
_____
_____
_____
_____

And I will do this by:

_____ (date)

Pray

Take a few moments to reflect on what you've learned today and over the course of session 5. Ask God to show you how your church can be a beacon of light in the community and a place where relationships are the motivation for reconciliation. Invite God to show your church community how to accept the task and take responsibility of building relationships through confession, repentance, and action. Thank God for his desire for healing, for his hearts toward relationships, and for his love for your community.

_____
_____
_____
_____
_____
_____

For Next Week: Read chapter 6 in *How to Fight Racism* and use the space below to write any insights or questions from your personal study that you want to discuss at the next group meeting.

_____
_____
_____
_____
_____
_____
_____

Journal, Reflections, and Notes

_____
_____
_____
_____
_____
_____
_____
_____
_____
_____
_____

HOW TO MAKE FRIENDS

*Let's be more intentional about learning how people
from different backgrounds see the world in ways I
never have because of my race or ethnicity.*
—JEMAR TISBY

Welcome

Welcome to session 6 of *How to Fight Racism*. As human beings, we desire connection and mutuality in friendships. The desire for human connection hardly could have been more apparent than during the novel coronavirus pandemic of 2020. When we could not be physically present with people because of health concerns, many of us realized how much we needed relationships and connection. But under ordinary conditions, our society is often so fragmented and individualized that it obscures our foundational desire for meaningful association with others. If anything good has come out of the pandemic of 2020, hopefully it encouraged us to remember that making friends across racial and ethnic lines can be as simple as asking, "Can we talk sometime?" And speaking of making friends, ask almost anyone for suggestions about what to do about racism, and most people will say we need relationships with people who are different from us. Cross-cultural friendships are one of the most obvious ways to move further down the road of racial justice. According to the ARC of Racial Justice, we build better relationships when we offer friendship to people who are different from us, and when we do so in a way that honors their story and identity as well as engages us in the potentially uncomfortable work of listening to and learning from one another. This is an indispensable aspect of continuing the journey of racial justice when we cultivate racially and ethnically diverse relationships in our lives. But hear me when I say that having one or two Black friends will not "fix" racism in your life. Adhering to a routine that takes you from majority-white setting to majority-white setting will never put you in a position to interact with people of color in any way beyond the most transactional encounters. You have to break out of your racially homogenous bubble. So let me suggest developing a community of friends with people from all different places and walks of life. This will not only help you be a better friend, but it will help you be more aware of what's required collectively on the journey toward racial justice.

Share

Take a few minutes to discuss one of the following statements:

- Consider your circle of friends. What percentage of friends are similar to you (age, gender, ethnicity, cultural background, etc.), and what percentage are different from you?
  —or—
- Where do you go to meet and interact with people who are different from you?

Watch

Play the video segment for session 6. As you watch, use the following outline to record any thoughts or concepts that stand out to you.

Notes
How to Make Friends

"The Dos and Don'ts of Reconciliation" by Thabiti Anyabwile (2015).
The key question of reconciliation: *Will you be my friend?*

Essential Understandings
1. Humility, Not Utility

Each and every person is worthy of being known.
Would I still be friends with this person if the topic of race never came up?

2. Listen More than You Speak: These Conversations Are Not New to Black People and People of Color

If you're in the racial majority, be prepared to hear "no" or "not yet" due to the exhaustion of people of color.

3. Racism Is Felt

It's visceral, not just an abstract, intellectual concept for debate.

> *When Black people and other people of color talk about race, we are uncovering old wounds, old traumas; it comes with smells and tastes and touch. And so to reveal that once again is difficult.*
> —JEMAR TISBY

The best way to approach racism is with:
- Empathy
- Solidarity
- An open mind

Racial Justice Practices

1. Do Your Homework First

Google it.
Own your ignorance.

2. Simplify It: Who Should I Ask to Be a Friend?

- Start by asking someone close to you: *How do you approach the topic of race?*
- Be direct: *Would you be willing to talk to me about your experiences?*
- But don't ambush people with the topic of race.

3. Put Yourself in a Position to Encounter People Who Are Different from You

Break up your patterns.
Get involved in your community, not just at church.
Change where you go for personal and professional services.

4. How to Talk to Racial Justice Resisters:

- *What do you do about them?*
- *How do you interact with them?*

---

*Three Considerations for Approaching
People with Whom You Disagree*

1. Decide whether the topic is worth engaging.
2. Don't patronize people.
3. Offer to trade information.

— EMMA FRANCES BLOOMFIELD, UNIVERSITY OF NEVADA, LAS VEGAS

Jemar's Suggestions
- Start with the Bible or something familiar.
- Talk about history.
- They have the opportunity to make a decision.

*For our struggle is not against flesh and blood, but against the
rulers, against the authorities, against the powers of this dark world
and against the spiritual forces of evil in the heavenly realms.*
— EPHESIANS 6:12

We have to recognize that what we're dealing with goes beyond the informational level to the spiritual level, to the soul level.

5. Find Your Community or Make One

*We cannot be on this journey of racial justice alone.
We cannot fight a solo fight against racism.*
— JEMAR TISBY

Find a place that affirms your identity without question.
**The ARC of Racial Justice compels us to pursue relationships
across racial and ethnic lines.**

Discuss

Take a few minutes with your group members to discuss what you just
watched and explore these concepts in Scripture.

1. What stood out to you from Jemar's teaching on how to make friends?

_____

_____

_____

2. Have you ever been at a place where you've given up or wanted to give up on relationships and friendships due to racial and ethnic tension? *Briefly share* the circumstance and the outcome.

_____

_____

_____

3. Consider what Jemar meant by the essential understanding "Humility, not Utility." Have you ever kept a friendship because it "looked good" for you to have someone who was of a different ethnicity as a friend? Would you still call that person your friend if the topic of race never came up?

_____

_____

_____

4. How have you *felt* racism?

_____

_____

_____

5. Which one of the racial justice practices do you need to work on the most, and why?

_____

_____

_____

_____

6. Which racial justice practice comes easiest to you, and which one is the most challenging? Explain why.

_____

_____

_____

7. How have you handled racial justice resisters? Or how have you been a racial justice resister? How does Jemar's teaching encourage you to respond in a different way?

_____

_____

_____

8. As Jemar suggested, have you found a place, a community, that affirms your identity without question? What would it take for this particular group or faith community to be that kind of safe place for you?

_____

_____

_____

Pray

Pray as a group before you close your time together. Ask God to help you develop friendships beyond your homogenous bubble—friends who are different from you. And if you are a person of color searching for a community where your dignity and humanity is affirmed, ask God to show you where to find that community, or ask this community to be that safe space for you and pray about it together. Use this space to keep track of prayer requests and group updates.

_____

_____

_____

_____

_____

_____

BETWEEN-SESSIONS PERSONAL STUDY

Weekly Reflection

Before you begin the between-sessions exercises, briefly review your video notes for session 6. In the space below, write down the *most significant point* you took away from this session.

_____

_____

_____

_____

_____

Diving Deeper: Essential Understandings

Reflect on the essential understandings Jemar provided in the video teaching, as well as the additional content for each of these essential understandings found in chapter 6 of *How to Fight Racism*. You may want to review the notes you took during the teaching session regarding each essential understanding as you read the corresponding questions.

1. Humility, Not Utility

A friendship based solely on what the other person can give you and what you can wrest from your connection is not a friendship; it's a series of exploitative engagements. Ask yourself, "Would I pursue friendship with this person if their race never came up in outside conversations?"

What else stood out to you about this essential understanding from Jemar's teaching in the video and from this chapter in *How to Fight Racism*?

_____

_____

_____

_____

_____

_____

_____

_____

_____

_____

How does this understanding change your view of the world around you?

_____

_____

_____

_____

_____

2. Listen More Than You Speak

White people need to be sensitive to the fact that although racial conversations may be new to them, they are not new to people of color. At the prospect of having yet another conversation about race, many people of color have honestly exclaimed, "We tired!"

What else stood out to you about this essential understanding from Jemar's teaching in the video and from this chapter in *How to Fight Racism*?

_____

_____

_____

_____

_____

_____

_____

_____

_____

How does this understanding change your view of the world around you?

_____

_____

_____

_____

3. Race Is Felt

For certain communities where racism has wrought untold damage, talking about racism is personal and visceral for members of these groups. It comes with smells, tastes, sounds, sights, and physical sensations. It carries with it injury, pride, and perseverance.

What else stood out to you about this essential understanding from Jemar's teaching in the video and from this chapter in _How to Fight Racism_?

_____

_____

_____

_____

_____

_____

How does this understanding change your view of the world around you?

_____

_____

_____

_____

Taking Action: Racial Justice Practices

Reflect on the racial justice practices Jemar provided in the video teaching, as well as the additional content for each of these practices found in chapter 6 of _How to Fight Racism_. You may want to review the notes you took during the teaching session regarding each racial justice practice as you read the corresponding questions.

1. Do Your Homework First

If you want to know about someone's racial and ethnic experience, first take the time and make the effort to learn what you can on your own. As one tired Black woman put it, "This information is already out there. There are so many resources that exist. If you are serious about hating and ending racism, you will put in the effort to find them. If you love me, do your homework." The person sitting across from you should not be your sole source of knowledge about race because:

- *They could have wrong or idiosyncratic views that are not representative of the majority of people.*
- *To be treated as the repository of all things racial is an unfair burden to put on anyone.*
- *Doing research beforehand demonstrates a minimum level of investment in the relationship as you take ownership of your own ignorance instead of expecting someone else to do it for you.*

What else stood out to you about this racial justice practice from Jemar's teaching in the video and from this chapter in *How to Fight Racism*?

_____

_____

_____

_____

_____

_____

_____

_____

_____

_____

_____

_____

How does this understanding change your view of the world around you?

_____

_____

_____

_____

_____

2. Who Should I Ask to Be a Friend? Can We Be Friends?

In pursuit of friendships with people from a range of racial and ethnic backgrounds, the simplest route is often the most effective. Simply ask someone if they want to talk—this can be a surprisingly effective practice in helping us get to know people who are different. When seeking meaningful friendships across racial and ethnic lines, consider these suggestions:

- *Start with your existing network of relationships—you may find you know people with an array of experiences, ages, and cultural backgrounds.*
- *Move from shallow understanding to expansive empathy with someone you already know by inviting that person to a meeting and saying, "Tell me about yourself."*
- *When speaking with a new friend or talking about race for the first time with an old friend, ask, "Would you be willing to share any of your experiences or views regarding race with me?"*

If you are Black or a person of color:

- *It's okay to acknowledge that talking to white people about race makes you want to recoil.*
- *Determine your boundaries—you are not obligated to satisfy anyone's curiosity on demand, so it's okay for you to choose the time, the place, and the way you will respond in conversation.*
- *Consider what telling your story can do for you.*

What else stood out to you about this racial justice practice from Jemar's teaching in the video and from this chapter in *How to Fight Racism*?

_____
_____
_____
_____
_____
_____
_____
_____
_____

How does this understanding change your view of the world around you?

_____

_____

_____

_____

_____

3. How to Meet People of Different Racial and Ethnic Backgrounds (Or Put Yourself in a Position to Encounter People Who Are Different from You)

To encounter people who are different from you, you will have to spend time at places in your community that have racial and ethnic diversity. This will help you go beyond your existing social network—which many seem obvious, and yet it's not a practice many people purposefully employ. Here are a few of Jemar's suggestions to meet others:

- _If you are physically active, join the local YMCA, YWCA, or community center instead of a private gym or club._
- _Get your hair cut at a different place._
- _Participate in free events around your community—a tax preparation class, a local book reading at the library, or a festival or parade celebrating people from a different racial and ethnic background._
- _Volunteer at multicultural events and festivities._

What else stood out to you about this racial justice practice from Jemar's teaching in the video and from this chapter in _How to Fight Racism_?

_____

_____

_____

_____

_____

_____

_____

How will you put this practice into action in your own life?

_____

_____

_____

_____

4. How to Talk to Racial Justice Resisters

Racial justice resisters are real. We all know someone who fits into this category. They might claim not to have a "racist bone in their body," but they remain steadfastly committed to denying the present reality of racism and not doing much to curb it.

Here are a few common deflections used by racial justice resisters:

- *"The people who keep talking about racism are the real racists."*
- *"The problem is that Black people (or another racial or ethnic group) want a handout and won't take advantage of their opportunities."*
- *"So-called experts are just liberals with an agenda."*

And here are a few suggestions on how to respond to racial justice resisters (by Emma Frances Bloomfield):

- *Decide whether the topic is worth engaging depending on the relationship—the strength of your relationship with a racial justice resister can help you estimate the likelihood of persuading them.*
- *Don't patronize—a condescending tone kills the opportunity for genuine dialogue.*
- *Trade information—one way to puncture the misinformation bubble is to offer new sources of information.*

> **For our struggle is not against flesh and blood, but against the rulers, against the authorities, against the powers of this dark world and against the spiritual forces of evil in the heavenly realms.**
> **—EPHESIANS 6:12**

What else stood out to you about this racial justice practice from Jemar's teaching in the video and from this chapter in *How to Fight Racism*?

_____

_____

_____

_____

_____

_____

How will you put this practice into action in your own life?

_____

_____

_____

_____

_____

5. Find Your Community or Make One

With all of the attacks and accusations, the half-steps and missteps, the slow progress and sometimes the regress of the racial justice movement, it's a wonder most of us keep going. For Black people and people of color, it is especially imperative that you find a community of like-minded people who can affirm your dignity and encourage you on your journey. Ethnic-specific spaces have long provided the strength, expression, awareness, and sensitivity Black people and other people of color need to keep going in the face of racist headwinds. If you are in need of accepting community, consider looking for this kind of community:

- _In your local church_
- _Through text message groups_
- _In online social media forums_

What else stood out to you about this racial justice practice from Jemar's teaching in the video and from this chapter in _How to Fight Racism_?

_____

_____

_____

_____

_____

_____

_____

How will you put this practice into action in your own life?

_____

_____

_____

_____

_____

Be Specific: Your Next Step

What specific step will you take this week as a result of what you've learned and explored today? Pay attention to the areas where you felt most convicted as you moved through this material.

Consider this: If you're struggling to think of something on your own, *consider places and spaces where you could go to meet new friends with varied cultural backgrounds. Change up your pattern to frequent those places and spaces more often. And then be you, and let others be themselves too.*

As a result of what I learned in this session, I will:

_____

_____

_____

_____

And I will do this by:

_____ (date)

Pray

Take a few moments to reflect on what you've learned today and over the course of session 6. Invite God into your relationships. Ask God to show you areas in your life where you need to broaden your horizon of relationships and "rub shoulders" more often with people who are different from you. And if you're a person of color looking for a community of people who can affirm your dignity and encourage you on your journey, ask God to help you find this community. Thank God for his love for you, and God's desire for us to be in relationship with others who reflect the dignity of humanity and the image of God to one another. Use this space to write out your prayer or journal your thoughts.

_____

_____

_____

_____

_____

For Next Week: Read chapter 7 in *How to Fight Racism* and use the space below to write any insights or questions from your personal study that you want to discuss at the next group meeting.

_____
_____
_____
_____
_____
_____
_____
_____
_____

Journal, Reflections, and Notes

_____
_____
_____
_____
_____
_____
_____
_____
_____
_____
_____
_____
_____
_____
_____
_____
_____
_____
_____
_____
_____

HOW TO BUILD DIVERSE COMMUNITIES

A society that has done something special against the Negro
for hundreds of years must now do something special for him,
in order to equip him to compete on an equal basis.
—MARTIN LUTHER KING JR.

Welcome

Welcome to session 7 of *How to Fight Racism*. Too many people of color have entered majority white spaces only to find that they are valued for their presence but not their perspective. This means organizations and institutions may have an element of diversity but not true equity. It's as though people of color in these organizations and institutions are invited to the party, but the music is completely unfamiliar, and no one asks them to dance. Diversity is a laudable goal, but it is only one part of the work of racial justice. Equity and inclusion must be part of that equation too. What this means is every organization should pursue racial and ethnic diversity, but they should know that it will not be easy. A bad organizational plan or a lack of dedication to the journey of racial justice can erect more roadblocks than having never engaged in such efforts in the first place. In other words, the journey of racial justice takes hard work. And it takes a collaboration of diversity, equity, and inclusion. On the other side of these efforts is an organization that truly welcomes people from all racial and ethnic backgrounds, makes everyone feel like they have a voice in how business is conducted, and has an opportunity for success. And the effort is worth the outcome for those willing to do the hard work. Organizations that fail to make an ongoing commitment to listen and respond to the unique needs of different groups of people not only limit their ability to fulfill their mission, but they leave a trail of hurt and harm in their wake. This session highlights the many ways that any organization—not just churches or faith-based organizations—can pursue racial justice by practicing diversity, equity, and inclusion. In doing so, these organizations can become a healthy environment for all different kinds of people and an example for others to follow. And if you're not currently working within an organization, stay with us. This is practical information for your family, your community, and the way you show up in the world.

Share

Take a few minutes to discuss one of the following statements:

- What does *inclusion* mean to you when you hear the phrase "diversity and inclusion"?
  —*or*—
- Share an example of an organization or institution doing diversity and inclusion well.

Watch

Play the video segment for session 7. As you watch, use the following outline to record any thoughts or concepts that stand out to you.

Notes
Diversifying Organizations
    PWI: Predominantly White Institution

Essential Understandings
1. Diversity, Equity, and Inclusion

> *Diversity is where everyone is invited to the party.*
> *Equity means that everyone gets to contribute to the song list.*
> *Inclusion means that everyone has the opportunity to dance.*
>
> —ROBERT SELLERS, CHIEF DIVERSITY OFFICER,
> UNIVERSITY OF MICHIGAN

2. Make a Plan and Work the Plan

Having a plan gives you goals and measures to continue the conversation and push toward racial justice.

Affirmative action and "reverse racism."

> *For centuries, organizations and institutions*
> *systematically and intentionally excluded*
> *racial and ethnic minorities. If that's the case,*
> *then diversity, equity, and inclusion demand*
> *that you systematically and intentionally*
> *include racial and ethnic minorities.*
>
> **—JEMAR TISBY**

3. Form a Group Focused on Racial Justice

Center the group around a piece of content.
Build your awareness and knowledge of race, racism, and white supremacy.
Do your homework as a group.
Build relationships.

Racial Justice Practices

1. Start with Stories

Ask about personal stories:
- *Who are you?*
- *Where are you from?*
- *What are your hopes for the group?*
- *Why are you interested in a group focused on racial justice?*
- *What are your earliest memories of race?*
- *What is your racial autobiography?*

2. Build Diversity, Equity, and Inclusion into the DNA of Your Organization

It's easier to start with diversity, equity, and inclusion rather than to add them in later.
The "cake" metaphor
Build racial justice into your organization's:
- Founding documents
- Bylaws
- Vision statement

3. Adopt a Statement on Racial Justice

This is a declaration of intent, a declaration of desire.

This is about the process of getting there, not just the destination.

It forces individuals in the organization to think deeply about racial justice.

4. "Cluster Hire" Racial and Ethnic Minorities

This cuts down on *tokenism*—having racial and ethnic minorities for aesthetic reasons in your organization.

This unburdens the small number of individual minorities from being the only voice of representation.

Cluster hiring means hiring more than one person of color at a time.

> *Any efforts toward racial justice are going to require a reallocation of resources, especially financial resources. It's going to take an investment to change course. It will take an investment to build diversity, equity, and inclusion into an organization. But it's been done before, and you can do it too.*
> —JEMAR TISBY

5. Pursue Diversity Even Where There Is a Lack of Racial and Ethnic Diversity

Keep in mind:
- You still need to teach and prepare people in your organization about diversity, equity, and inclusion.
- You still need to acknowledge racial and ethnic minorities present in your organization, no matter how small the numbers or percentages.

When to leave:
- Are you suffering so much emotional and mental trauma that you're actually having physical health problems?
- Have your repeated attempts to bring up issues of racial equity and diversity not only been met with a lack of action but also with anger, aggressiveness, and defensiveness?
- Have you been given institutional authority to implement change?
- Have other racial and ethnic minorities had similar experiences?

Understand this: *Life moves in seasons.*

It's not just about what you're leaving;
it's about what you're moving toward.
—JEMAR TISBY

The ARC of Racial Justice means we have to have relationships across racial and ethnic lines, and organizations need to pursue diversity, equity, and inclusion.

Organizations that pursue diversity, equity, and inclusion can lead to flourishing of people within the organization and whatever cause or mission they serve.

Discuss

Take a few minutes with your group members to discuss what you just watched and explore these concepts in Scripture.

1. What stood out to you from Jemar's teaching on how to build diverse communities?

_____

_____

_____

_____

2. How would you describe the following terms after listening to today's teaching: *diversity*, *equity*, and *inclusion*?

_____

_____

_____

_____

3. On a scale from 1 to 10, with 1 being the lowest score and 10 being the highest, how would you rate the organization(s) where you work or serve in their attempts at diversity, equity, and inclusion? Why?

_____

_____

_____

_____

4. How would your colleagues, coworkers, and fellow volunteers of racial and ethnic minorities talk about their experience in your organization? If you are unsure, who will you ask about their personal and professional experience in your organization?

_____

_____

_____

_____

_____

5. What can you do personally or collectively to contribute to a healthier perspective of diversity, equity, and inclusion in your organization?

_____

_____

_____

_____

_____

6. Even if you're not in a position or place to influence the way your organization approaches racial justice, how are you building relationships and learning the stories of coworkers who are different from you, especially those who belong to racial and ethnic minority groups? How could you grow in this area of relationship-building?

_____

_____

_____

_____

_____

7. Does your organization have a statement on racial justice? If so, it might be helpful for you to know and share this statement. And if not, how can you help your organization establish a statement?

_____

_____

_____

_____

_____

8. How does your organization contribute to the flourishing of people and the mission they serve, and how does their stance on racial justice contribute to that flourishing? If they are not currently contributing to flourishing, particularly in areas of racial justice, share your vision of how the organization *could* contribute to this kind of flourishing. (If this is a hard question to answer, consider whether it might be time for you to leave.)

_____
_____
_____
_____
_____
_____

Pray

Pray as a group before you close your time together. Ask God to show you how each one of you can be a force for change in the organizations and institutions where you work, serve, and volunteer. If you work from home and care for your family, ask God to show you how this session relates to your current role at home. Use this space to keep track of prayer requests and group updates.

_____
_____
_____
_____
_____
_____
_____
_____
_____
_____
_____
_____

BETWEEN-SESSIONS PERSONAL STUDY

Weekly Reflection

Before you begin the between-sessions exercises, briefly review your video notes for session 7. In the space below, write down the *most significant point* you took away from this session.

_____

_____

_____

_____

Diving Deeper: Essential Understandings

Reflect on the essential understandings Jemar provided in the video teaching, as well as the additional content for each of these essential understandings found in chapter 7 of *How to Fight Racism*. You may want to review the notes you took during the teaching session regarding each essential understanding as you read the corresponding questions.

1. Diversity, Equity, and Inclusion

Here's the truth: the mere presence of racial variety does not produce racial justice. That's why there is a need to build diversity, equity, and inclusion into existing institutions. Diversity, equity, and inclusion are distinct principles, and all three are necessary for a healthy organizational culture. If diversity focuses on who is present, equity says who has access to a community's resources and on what terms, and inclusion speaks to the sense of welcome and belonging extended to each person or group.

What else stood out to you about this essential understanding from Jemar's teaching in the video and from this chapter in *How to Fight Racism*?

_____

_____

_____

_____

_____

How does this understanding change your view of the world around you?

_____

_____

_____

_____

2. Make a Plan and Work the Plan

It is not enough for organizations to just talk about diversity, equity, and inclusion, they must have a comprehensive plan for creating such a culture. And they must understand that engaging in half-hearted efforts at diversity can be more devastating than not doing anything at all. Loose efforts can lead to cynicism and confirm racial stereotypes. This is not helpful—and can in fact be harmful. That's why an effective, comprehensive plan is the priority.

What else stood out to you about this essential understanding from Jemar's teaching in the video and from this chapter in *How to Fight Racism*?

_____

_____

_____

_____

How does this understanding change your view of the world around you?

_____

_____

_____

_____

Taking Action: Racial Justice Practices

Now reflect on the racial justice practices Jemar provided in the video teaching, as well as the additional content for each of these practices found in chapter 7 of *How to Fight Racism*. You may want to review the notes you took during the teaching session regarding each racial justice practice as you read the corresponding questions.

1. Do a Group Study on Race: Start with Stories

While doing a group study on race might seem like an odd place to start, a book study or Bible study group on racial justice is actually one of the best ways to increase awareness *and* build relationships. The idea is to gather people from different perspectives around a piece of content for a consistent amount of time to dive into deeper levels of cross-cultural understanding. Here are key habits for doing a group study:

- *Cultivate diversity to the extent possible—race, ethnicity, age, gender, experience, and so on. You can invite specific people who represent a range of cultures to the group, or you can gather the list of interested participants and divide them up into diverse groups based on what you know about their cultural locations.*
- *Start with stories. Take time to build trust before diving into hard topics by inviting participants to talk about themselves. Asking the following questions humanizes each person:*
  - *What are your hopes for the group?*
  - *How did you first become interested in the topic of racial justice?*

What else stood out to you about this racial justice practice from Jemar's teaching in the video and from this chapter in *How to Fight Racism*?

_____

_____

_____

_____

_____

_____

_____

How does this understanding change your view of the world around you?

_____

_____

_____

_____

_____

2. Build Diversity, Equity, and Inclusion into the DNA of Your Organization

The truth is that the trajectory for many organizations might be drastically different today had they started with diversity as a priority. For too many leaders, racial and ethnic diversity has been treated like an elective class in high school or college—a "nice to have" option. Yet for healthy and inclusive organizations, diversity is a required part of the organizational education. The following racial justice practices are grouped here as a means of what it takes for an organization to build diversity, equity, and inclusion into their organizational DNA:

- *Build a case for "why." Don't assume everyone values racial diversity or is willing to take the necessary actions to achieve it, so build a case by explaining why diversity enhances the effectiveness of an organization.*
- *Assemble the team. Gather a team that will facilitate the comprehensive plan toward diversity, equity, and inclusion and make sure the team reflects the diversity to which the organization aspires.*

What else stood out to you about this racial justice practice from Jemar's teaching in the video and from this chapter in *How to Fight Racism*?

_____

_____

_____

_____

_____

_____

_____

_____

_____

_____

_____

How does this understanding change your view of the world around you?

_____

_____

_____

_____

_____

3. Adopt a Statement on Racial Justice

If your organization is committed to racial justice, then they should have a written statement that expresses their views. This message communicates two important messages to racial and ethnic minorities in your organization: (1) that the leadership is mindful of issues related to race, and (2) there is an official policy to appeal to if an incident occurs. But remember, a document on racial justice is not itself racial justice; it is the written expression of a desire, not the action of that desire.

Also, **require applicants to submit a statement on racial justice.** Have your potential hiring candidates write a statement or make a verbal explanation about their commitment to racial justice. In doing so, you will be aware of their cultural intelligence—their capacity to be aware of and sensitive to the various backgrounds of the people with whom they will interact.

What else stood out to you about this racial justice practice from Jemar's teaching in the video and from this chapter in _How to Fight Racism_?

_____

_____

_____

_____

_____

_____

_____

How will you put this practice into action in your own life?

_____

_____

_____

_____

_____

4. "Cluster Hire" Racial and Ethnic Minorities

If you want to demonstrate a commitment to racial justice, then your team will have to reflect more racial and ethnic diversity. Cluster hiring is an effective way of hiring several people at once who have overlapping interests and expertise in various departments and roles in an organization. Instead of heaping the burden of overcoming racial injustice on the back of a single person designated as the "diversity hire," a cluster of people who come in with the same mindset can help shift an organization's beliefs and practices and have a better chance at surviving in a predominantly white institution as well.

What else stood out to you about this racial justice practice from Jemar's teaching in the video and from this chapter in *How to Fight Racism*?

_____

_____

_____

_____

_____

_____

_____

How will you put this practice into action in your own life?

_____

_____

_____

_____

5. Pursuing Diversity Even If Your Organization Remains Homogenous

Sometimes organizations remain homogenous if the organization is located in a place that does not have much racial diversity or if there is a lack of zeal, knowledge, or sincerity in regard to moving toward racial diversity. But racially homogenous places can still find meaningful ways to pursue diversity. Here's how:

- *Equip your people. Teach the principles of diversity, equity, and inclusion because the people in your organization may move on one day to a space that's more diverse.*

- *Acknowledge that there is probably still some level of racial diversity in your organization—no matter how small.*
- *Remember there is all kinds of diversity beyond race and ethnicity—cultivate geographic, gender, and class diversity too.*
- *As an organization, you can support another organization that has more racial and ethnic diversity.*

What else stood out to you about this racial justice practice from Jemar's teaching in the video and from this chapter in *How to Fight Racism*?

_____
_____
_____
_____
_____
_____
_____

How will you put this practice into action in your own life?

_____
_____
_____
_____

6. When to Organize and When to Leave

For Black people and people of color it is not uncommon to find yourselves in predominantly white settings. Sometimes it's best to leave; however, sometimes you must stay. If you have to stay, understand there is strength in numbers when it comes to fighting racism. A chorus of voices is easier to hear than a lone voice, which is easy to silence. But also be aware of when the organization is damaging to your emotional and spiritual health, and you must go. Here are a few tips on when to stay and organize, and when to leave:

When to Stay and Organize
- *Look at your organization's grievance policy. It can provide valuable information on how to file a complaint if you're experiencing racial or ethnic discrimination.*

- *Gather a group of others who are willing to share any experiences of racial or ethnic discrimination along with yours. Write letters or emails or meet with management.*
- *Have a list of specific outcomes and changes you want to see in the organization.*

When to Leave

- *Are you suffering so much emotional and mental trauma that you are having health problems?*
- *Have your repeated attempts to bring up issues of racial equity and diversity not only been met with a lack of action but with anger and aggressiveness?*
- *Have you attempted to bring up your concerns using the approved mechanisms for filing grievances?*
- *Does the organization have a stated plan for diversity, equity, and inclusion to which you can hold leaders accountable?*
- *Have you been given institutional authority to implement changes?*
- *Have other racial and ethnic minorities had similar experiences?*

What else stood out to you about this racial justice practice from Jemar's teaching in the video and from this chapter in *How to Fight Racism***?**

_____

_____

_____

_____

_____

_____

_____

_____

_____

_____

How will you put this practice into action in your own life?

_____

_____

_____

_____

_____

Be Specific: Your Next Step

What specific step will you take this week as a result of what you've learned and explored today? Pay attention to the areas where you felt most convicted as you moved through this material.

Consider this: If you're struggling to think of something on your own, *consider how you can contribute to the health of your organization by championing one or two of the racial justice practices from this session. What can you do with your time and your consistent effort to make your organization (or your family or community) a healthy place for all?*

As a result of what I learned in this session, I will:

_____
_____
_____
_____
_____
_____
_____

And I will do this by:
_____ (date)

Pray

Take a few moments to reflect on what you've learned today and over the course of session 7. Invite God into your work experiences (or wherever you spend the majority of your intellectual energy with your physical presence). Ask God to show you areas in your organization that are in need of repair when it comes to diversity, equity, and inclusion. Ask God to show you how to be a part of the change needed for racial justice. If you are a racial or ethnic minority in a racist or hostile work environment, ask God to give you the courage to stay and help make a change or the freedom to go as you seek emotional and spiritual health. Thank God for his love for you and God's desire for us to be in relationship with others in our workplaces, organizations, and institutions who are on the journey of racial justice. Use this space to write out your prayer or journal your thoughts.

_____
_____
_____
_____
_____
_____
_____

For Next Week: Read chapter 8 in *How to Fight Racism* and use the space below to write any insights or questions from your personal study that you want to discuss at the next group meeting.

_____
_____
_____
_____
_____
_____
_____

Journal, Reflections, and Notes

_____
_____
_____
_____
_____
_____
_____
_____
_____

HOW TO WORK FOR RACIAL JUSTICE

*You cannot love your neighbor while supporting or accepting
systems that crush, exploit, and dehumanize them.*

—MIKA EDMONDSON

Welcome

Welcome to session 8 of *How to Fight Racism*. It is one matter to acknowledge that all people are made equal and have inherent dignity in their very being. It is another matter to identify the ways the image of God is defaced in individuals through systems and policies and then to work against those injustices. If Christians claim to be *for* their neighbors, then they must also be concerned about the structures and systems that enable or inhibit their neighbors' flourishing. In a beloved community, as Martin Luther King Jr. said, love is an action that uses levers of power to bring about justice. However, many Christians maintain the idea that they should not get involved in matters of public justice, and this separation leaves people both outside and inside the circles of Christianity wondering how you can talk about love without talking about justice. Unfortunately, many white Christians have become de facto defenders of the unjust status quo. And their reasoning for doing so is multi-faceted. Some claim matters of justice are "too political," others claim modern day matters of justice are built on secular philosophies such as Marxism and communism, and still others fail to see matters of justice as systemic issues that need to be addressed in the broad structures of society. Without love there can be no justice. Jesus encapsulated the core of Christianity as love for God and love for neighbor. This love animates the call for racial justice.

Love is the fiery heartbeat at the center of the urgent call for justice in our world. Love is the energizing force of justice that insists on fairness and equity for all. Love is the motivating factor that demolishes any paternalistic attitudes and builds a posture of humble service. So in this session we will talk about matters of public justice rooted in love of neighbor as we continue to explore the ARC of Racial Justice. This includes looking at how churches and faith communities can commit to changing racist policies too.

Share

Take a few minutes to discuss one of the following statements:

- How does the Greatest Commandment guide your life? *Love God with all your heart, soul, mind and strength, and love your neighbor as yourself* (Mark 12:30–31, summarized).
  —*or*—
- What does love require of you?

Watch

Play the video segment for session 8. As you watch, use the following outline to record any thoughts or concepts that stand out to you.

Notes
The Montgomery Bus Boycott—381 Days

> *But we must remember as we boycott that a boycott is not an end within itself; . . . the end is reconciliation; the end is redemption; the end is the creation of the beloved community.*
> —MARTIN LUTHER KING JR.

Essential Understandings
Love Is an Action

> *Power, properly understood, is the ability to achieve purpose. It is the strength required to bring about social,*

political, or economic changes. . . . Power at its best is love
implementing the demands of justice. Justice at its best
is love correcting everything that stands against love.
—MARTIN LUTHER KING JR., *WHERE DO WE GO*
FROM HERE: CHAOS OR COMMUNITY?

Love Demands Justice

Justice concerns:
- interpersonal interactions of individuals
- systems and institutions

You cannot love your neighbor while supporting or accepting
systems that crush, exploit, or dehumanize them.
—MIKA EDMONDSON

Without Love There Can Be No Justice

One of the teachers of the law came and heard them debating.
Noticing that Jesus had given them a good answer, he asked him,
"Of all the commandments, which is the most important?"

"The most important one," answered Jesus, "is this:
'Hear, O Israel: The Lord our God, the Lord is one. Love the
Lord your God with all your heart and with all your soul
and with all your mind and with all your strength.'
The second is this: 'Love your neighbor as yourself.'
There is no commandment greater than these."
—MARK 12:28–31

Love of God and Love of Neighbor

Ain't no such thing as I can hate anyone
and hope to see the face of God.
—FANNIE LOU HAMER

Love as the Motivation to Do Justice
Justice is the witness to Jesus.

Truly I tell you, whatever you did for one of the least of these brothers and sisters of mine, you did for me.

—MATTHEW 25:40

Racial Justice Practices

1. Steward Your Budget for Justice

- Raise money for other religious organizations, particularly minority-led ones.
- Use your financial resources to help neighborhood organizations doing similar work.
- Allow community organizations to use your building when it's not being used.

2. Cast Your Vote

- Host a discussion forum. Be a gathering space for the community.
- Host a voter registration drive.

Voting is a fundamental civil right.

—JEMAR TISBY

3. Utilize Your Existing Racial Justice Documents

- Do a preaching or teaching series.
- Form a committee to implement an action plan.

4. Freedom School

- Educate the next generation about justice.

5. Partner with a Local Public School

- Ask what the needs are for local schools and find out where schools need the most support.
- Do not assume the needs without getting input from school personnel.
- Consider mentoring.
- Start a sports team or a hobby-oriented club as needed.
- Support the teachers and school staff to show appreciation.

It's not a matter of *if* churches should show love as an expression of public justice, it's *how* they should get involved.

Discuss

Take a few minutes with your group members to discuss what you just watched and explore these concepts in Scripture.

1. What stood out to you from Jemar's teaching on how to work for racial justice?

    _____

    _____

    _____

    _____

2. How have you experienced love as justice and justice as love?

    _____

    _____

    _____

    _____

    _____

3. Read Mark 12:28–34. As Christians, how does the Greatest Commandment inform the way we love in public, and how does it propel us toward justice?

    _____

    _____

    _____

    _____

4. What would you say to a fellow Christian or a church community who pushes the idea of love and yet refuses to take a stand on justice? What are the implications of these kinds of actions—of pushing love without standing for justice?

    _____

    _____

    _____

    _____

5. How could your church or your family steward your budget for justice?
What are some practical ways this could be accomplished? Start small;
think big.

_____

_____

_____

_____

_____

_____

6. Why is it important to cast your vote? And how can you do this in
a bipartisan way that encourages the idea of voting regardless of
party lines?

_____

_____

_____

7. How is your church utilizing your statement of racial justice or existing
documents and statements of justice and love? If little is being done,
then consider a few practical ways you could encourage your church
leadership to teach, preach, and practice justice in love for the benefit
of the entire community.

_____

_____

_____

8. How is your church contributing to local freedom school opportunities
as well as local public school support? If little is being done, make a
list of a few practical steps your church could take toward supporting
educational opportunities for the youth in your local community and
expressing appreciation to educators who are serving those youth.

_____

_____

_____

_____

_____

_____

Pray

Pray as a group before you close your time together. Ask God to open your hearts and minds to the areas around you where love needs to penetrate the systems and structures of our society as justice so that *all* of us may have the opportunity to flourish. Invite God to show you how to love your neighbors well as individuals and as a faith community. Use this space to keep track of prayer requests and group updates.

_____

_____

_____

_____

_____

_____

_____

_____

_____

_____

_____

_____

_____

_____

_____

_____

_____

_____

_____

_____

_____

_____

_____

_____

_____

_____

_____

_____

_____

_____

_____

BETWEEN-SESSIONS PERSONAL STUDY

Weekly Reflection

Before you begin the between-sessions exercises, briefly review your video notes for session 8. In the space below, write down the *most significant point* you took away from this session.

_____

_____

_____

_____

Diving Deeper: Essential Understandings

Reflect on the essential understandings Jemar provided in the video teaching, as well as the additional content for each of these essential understandings found in chapter 8 of *How to Fight Racism*. You may want to review the notes you took during the teaching session regarding each essential understanding as you read the corresponding questions.

1. Love for God and for Neighbor

Jesus summarized the most important commands of the Christian faith with a simple remark called the Greatest Commandment. That is, "'Love the Lord your God with all your heart and with all your soul and with all your mind and with all your strength.' The second is this: 'Love your neighbor as yourself'" (Mark 12:29–31). Notice that Jesus juxtaposes love for God with love for neighbor. Jesus distinguishes between loving God and loving others, yet he does not separate the two. Love of God is demonstrated through love of others.

What else stood out to you about this essential understanding from Jemar's teaching in the video and from this chapter in *How to Fight Racism*?

_____

_____

_____

_____

_____

_____

_____

How does this understanding change your view of the world around you?

_____

_____

_____

_____

2. Fighting Racism Is Bearing Witness to Christ

Some Christians have attempted to insert a wedge between the task of evangelism—proclaiming the good news about Jesus Christ and the salvation he offers—and the task of racial justice. This is a false dichotomy. Love for God and love for neighbor mean that preaching the gospel and working for racial justice are not at odds; each one needs the other. In Acts 1:8, Jesus Christ called his followers to bear witness about him throughout the world. And in Matthew 25:40, Jesus says, "Truly I tell you, whatever you did for one of the least of these brothers and sisters of mine, you did for me."

What else stood out to you about this essential understanding from Jemar's teaching in the video and from this chapter in *How to Fight Racism*?

_____

_____

_____

_____

_____

How does this understanding change your view of the world around you?

_____

_____

_____

_____

Taking Action: Racial Justice Practices

Now reflect on the racial justice practices Jemar provided in the video teaching, as well as the additional content for each of these practices found in chapter 8 of *How to Fight Racism*. You may want to review the notes you took during the teaching session regarding each racial justice practice as you read the corresponding questions.

1. Steward Your Budget for Justice

Many racial justice practices include a redistribution of money because racism has always been closely related to economic exploitation and greed. The point of this practice is not to ascribe a monetary value to racism or racial justice but to acknowledge and address the clear financial dimensions of discrimination. Here's what this could look like for your church:

- *Instead of doing a capital campaign to raise funds for a new building, your church might use that money to help local nonprofits and other churches.*
- *Take up a special offering or collection to support another church.*
- *Host a community organization or another congregation in your church facility free of charge.*
- *Spend less on internal programs and allocate that money for community organizations.*

What else stood out to you about this racial justice practice from Jemar's teaching in the video and from this chapter in *How to Fight Racism*?

_____

_____

_____

_____

_____

How does this understanding change your view of the world around you?

_____

_____

_____

_____

2. Cast Your Vote

Churches on the margins tend to have an easier time integrating faith and justice because they have endured the effects of injustice firsthand. Much of the Black church tradition distinguishes between the mission of the church and the workings of political bodies, but they have always seen the interrelatedness of the two in the cause of justice. According to the Internal Revenue Service (IRS), churches cannot endorse or participate in campaigns for any particular candidates, parties, or platforms if they want to maintain their tax-exempt status. But that doesn't mean churches have to stay silent on issues of justice or opt out of encouraging people to cast their vote as a civil liberty. The following racial justice practices are grouped here as ways of participating in the voting process:

- _**Host a Candidate Forum.**_ _It is possible for your church to host a candidate forum without endorsing particular individuals or parties by fostering respectful dialogue and responsible information sharing with all candidates._
- _**Host a Voter Registration Drive.**_ _Voting is one of the most fundamental rights of an individual in a democracy, but having access to voice one's priorities and perspectives in a democracy is often an issue. You promote voting rights broadly without pressure to promote a certain policy or candidate._

What else stood out to you about this racial justice practice from Jemar's teaching in the video and from this chapter in _How to Fight Racism_?

_____

_____

_____

_____

_____

_____

How does this understanding change your view of the world around you?

_____

_____

_____

_____

3. Utilize Existing Church Documents

Many churches and denominations have existing statements on racial justice and racial reconciliation. And if they don't, now is the time to craft these statements. But for these statements to have any power, they must reflect and inform the living narrative of a congregation or an organization. This may include the following:

- *Do an entire preaching or teaching series based on existing church documents regarding race relations.*
- *Compose Bible study lessons about race relations based on Scripture passages cited in the church documents.*
- *Host a special event around a particular church document on race relations and include a keynote address, a panel discussion, and a time for questions and answers.*
- *Form a local congregational committee to determine how best to implement the ideas and recommendations contained in the church documents.*
- *Start a community development corporation (CDC). This is a racial justice practice that many churches do to foster justice in their neighborhoods and cities. A CDC is a nonprofit organization formed to meet the needs of the local community, and it is an effective way for a church to live out their desire for race relations in their community.*

What else stood out to you about this racial justice practice from Jemar's teaching in the video and from this chapter in _How to Fight Racism_?

_____

_____

_____

_____

_____

_____

_____

How will you put this practice into action in your own life?

_____

_____

_____

_____

4. Host a Freedom School

Freedom schools are voluntary, short-term schools that take place when regular school is not in session. They teach academic skills and provide tools necessary to pursue racial justice. When churches host freedom schools, they have the opportunity to educate young people about a biblical view of diversity, race, and ethnicity. They can explain the responsibility of Christians to love their neighbors through acts of justice. The emphasis in freedom school is on discussion of important racial justice issues rather than lecture and passive consumption of content. And the goal is to instill in youth a sense of collective responsibility for their community. Hosting a freedom school involves:

- *Creating curriculum*
- *Training instructors*
- *Financial budgeting*

What else stood out to you about this racial justice practice from Jemar's teaching in the video and from this chapter in *How to Fight Racism*?

_____

_____

_____

_____

_____

_____

_____

_____

_____

How will you put this practice into action in your own life?

_____

_____

_____

_____

5. Sponsor a Local Public School

Few institutions are rooted in the community as deeply as public schools. If you want to better know your neighborhood, your city, and the people in it, getting involved in schools is one of the best ways to do it. And the primary concern for churches getting involved in local public schools should be to serve the school and the students. But the church will also benefit by learning helpful information about their community as they spend time with students, teachers, and staff and by having more cross-cultural interactions through meaningful, personal relationships. And the needs in public schools are great. Just make sure the leadership of your church reaches out to local school personnel to *ask* about the critical needs of the school and the community before *assuming* the answers and moving to action.

What else stood out to you about this racial justice practice from Jemar's teaching in the video and from this chapter in *How to Fight Racism*?

_____

_____

_____

_____

_____

_____

_____

_____

_____

_____

How will you put this practice into action in your own life?

_____

_____

_____

Be Specific: Your Next Step

What specific step will you take this week as a result of what you've learned and explored today? Pay attention to the areas where you felt most convicted as you moved through this material.

Consider this: If you're struggling to think of something on your own, *consider how you can contribute to meeting the needs of your local community through your involvement in your church or faith community. Is there something the church is already doing to meet those needs, and you could join the effort?*

As a result of what I learned in this session, I will:

_____

_____

_____

_____

_____

_____

And I will do this by:

_____ (date)

Pray

Take a few moments to reflect on what you've learned today and over the course of session 8. Invite God into the work of racial justice in your faith community. Ask God to show the leaders of your church where and how they can best meet the critical needs of the community. Ask God to show your church how to put love in action through justice. Thank God for the ways he's uniquely positioned your church to participate in the positive transformation of your community and the ways your church has the opportunity to break down walls of bigotry and build bridges of equity. Use this space to write out your prayer or journal your thoughts.

_____

_____

_____

_____

_____

_____

_____

_____

_____

_____

For Next Week: Read chapter 9 in *How to Fight Racism* and use the space below to write any insights or questions from your personal study that you want to discuss at the next group meeting.

_____

_____

_____

_____

_____

_____

_____

_____

Journal, Reflections, and Notes

_____

_____

_____

_____

_____

_____

_____

_____

_____

_____

_____

_____

_____

_____

_____

_____

_____

_____

_____

HOW TO FIGHT SYSTEMIC RACISM

Justice is what love looks like in public.

—CORNEL WEST

Welcome

Welcome to session 9 of *How to Fight Racism*. Residential segregation, abusive policing practices, and generational poverty are inequalities that cannot be attributed to the actions of a few individuals or supposed pathologies of people of color. They are the same inequalities that existed in Ferguson, Missouri, in 2014—the year a Black eighteen-year-old named Mike Brown was shot by police. And the reason we face this widespread racial inequality is due to systems—political, educational, cultural, economic—that have been set up to support it. Fighting racism means looking at the operating system of our society and evaluating which protocols are creating or perpetuating racial justice. Because there is no such thing as a race-neutral policy. According to Ibram X. Kendi, every policy is "producing or sustaining either racial inequality or equity between racial groups." But the logical extensions of the Christian ethic of love is justice and advocacy for the public good. And this is accomplished through collective efforts of systemic change, not just our individual actions. For far too long, the discussion about race has focused on the intentions and feelings of individuals, and this has allowed people to sidestep the necessity of addressing systemic racism. Confronting the interlocking patterning of practices and policies that create and maintain racial inequalities is what love looks like in public. This session offers insight on how to fight systemic racism in the structure of our society as we continue to explore the ARC of Racial Justice.

Share

Take a few minutes to discuss one of the following statements:

- Define systemic racism.

  —*or*—

- How have you witnessed or experienced systemic racism collectively in society?

Watch

Play the video segment for session 9. As you watch, use the following outline to record any thoughts or concepts that stand out to you.

Notes
The Killing of Mike Brown in Ferguson, MO (2014)

Racial Justice
Patterns of Policing

Essential Understandings
1. Racism Is Not Just about Individual Behavior—It Has to Do with Systems and Policies
UNDERSTANDING POVERTY

> *53% of White Evangelicals blamed poverty on lack of effort. 64% of Black Christians attributed poverty more to their circumstances.*
>
> —*WASHINGTON POST* AND THE KAISER
> FAMILY FOUNDATION

The partisan divide in understanding poverty:
- Among Democrats: *26 percent blamed a lack of effort, while 72 percent blamed circumstances.*
- Among Republicans: *63 percent blamed a lack of effort, while 32 percent blamed circumstances.*

POLICIES, NOT JUST PEOPLE, CAN PERPETUATE RACISM

> *A racist policy is any measure that produces or*
> *sustains racial inequality between racial groups. . . .*
> *By policy, I mean written and unwritten laws, rules,*
> *procedures, processes, regulations, and guidelines that*
> *govern people. There is no such thing as a race-neutral*
> *policy. Every policy is producing or sustaining either*
> *racial inequity or equity between racial groups.*
> —IBRAM X. KENDI, *HOW TO BE ANTIRACIST* (2019)

Fighting racism requires:
- Looking at the operating system of a society
- Evaluating which protocols or policies are leading to greater equity or inequity

2. It's about Impact, Not Intent
What matters is the impact, the effect on people.

3. What's Worth Conserving?

Racial Justice Practices
1. Advocate for Voting Rights
- For those who are incarcerated
- For the restoration of the "preclearance clause"

On Election Days, we can:
- Provide transportation
- Provide information
- Volunteer at polling stations

On a national level, we can:
- Make it easier to vote
- Vote on the weekend
- Make voting a national holiday
- Automatic voting registration at age eighteen

2. Work on Immigration Reform

- Start by using helpful language, such as "undocumented" instead of "illegal."
- Protect the Deferred Action for Childhood Arrivals Act (DACA).
- Establish a pathway to citizenship for people who are already here.
- Do away with the US Immigration and Customs Enforcement (ICE) division.
- Extend healthcare to undocumented immigrants.
- Close detention centers.

3. Pay Reparations

Make up for:

- Missed payment to laborers in chattel slavery
- Rescinded land ownership
- Exploitation of laborers, landowners, and soldiers of color

The racial wealth gap:

> **As of 2016, the median household wealth of Black families was just one-tenth of White households.**
>
> **—WILLIAM A. DARITY JR. AND A. KIRSTEN MULLEN,**
> ***FROM HERE TO EQUALITY* (2020)**

Reparations as economic justice.

This has been done before:

- 2020 coronavirus relief package
- German reparations to Holocaust survivors
- US reparations to Japanese-Americans

How to Support and Promote Reparations

- Support the HR-40 bill to establish a study commission to see what paying reparations might look like.
- Support historically Black colleges and universities.
- Offer reparations pricing to support organizations that predominantly employ and serve the Black community.
- Support Black-led organizations and institutions financially and with in-kind donations.

Reparation means "repair."

4. Criminal Justice Reform

George Stinney was executed at age fourteen (1944)

> *Since 1973, more than 165 who had been sentenced
> to death row were later found to be innocent.*
> —DEATH PENALTY INFORMATION CENTER

- Abolish the death penalty.
- Eliminate cash bail.
- Overhaul police policies and put funds toward preventative measures.

5. Promote Equitable Funding for Public Schools

- Redraw lines so districts are integrated both ethnically and economically.
- Completely revise our funding scheme so that schools have a more equitable distribution of financial resources.

And more Racial Justice Practices include: *healthcare, housing, environment.*

> *The ARC of Racial Justice says that the
> commitment portion means recognizing
> that commitment means understanding that
> racism works itself out in more than just
> personal attitudes, but in policies that can
> create and perpetuate racial inequality.*
> —JEMAR TISBY

Confronting these interlocking patterns and policies that create racial inequality is what love looks like in public.

Discuss

Take a few minutes with your group members to discuss what you just watched and explore these concepts in Scripture.

1. What stood out to you from Jemar's teaching on how to love in public?

_____

_____

_____

2. How have you personally experienced or witnessed racism in the form of a system or policy?

_____

_____

_____

3. Why do you think it's so hard for predominantly white communities to see racism embedded in systems and policies and not just as the result or intention of individual behavior?

_____

_____

_____

4. Jemar gave us a hefty list of racial justice practices for how to fight racism and love in public. Why are some of these practices considered "controversial"?

_____

_____

_____

5. Which practice creates the most tension for you? Why? What else do you need to understand the importance of this suggestion as a racial justice practice?

_____

_____

_____

_____

6. Which practice do you feel most passionate about, and why? How are you contributing to this practice as an individual and as a community?

_____

_____

_____

7. What are a few steps you could take in two or three of these racial justice practices to show "love in public" this week?

_____

_____

_____

8. How does your church contribute to the notion that showing "love in public" means understanding how racism is perpetuated in policies and systems, not just individual behaviors? If your church is lacking in this area, what suggestions do you have for how your church leadership can step up their game to "love in public" using some of these racial justice practices?

_____

_____

_____

_____

_____

_____

Pray

Pray as a group before you close your time together. Ask God to open your hearts and minds to the systemic racism around you, and ask God to show you specific ways you can practice your commitment to racial justice as you speak about these systemic issues and show love through justice in public. Use this space to keep track of prayer requests and group updates.

_____

_____

_____

_____

_____

_____

_____

_____

_____

_____

BETWEEN-SESSIONS PERSONAL STUDY

Weekly Reflection

Before you begin the between-sessions exercises, briefly review your video notes for session 9. In the space below, write down the *most significant point* you took away from this session.

_____

_____

_____

_____

_____

Diving Deeper: Essential Understandings

Reflect on the essential understandings Jemar provided in the video teaching, as well as the additional content for each of these essential understandings found in chapter 9 of *How to Fight Racism*. You may want to review the notes you took during the teaching session regarding each essential understanding as you read the corresponding questions.

1. It's Not Just about Individual Behavior

Some people believe that people who are poor are simply lazy or unmotivated. In fact, the data shows that many groups still think of society-wide issues—such as poverty—in individual terms, as a matter that depends more on personal behaviors than policies and systems. But what is needed is a focus that takes into account the individual's circumstances while also taking action to combat the underlying systemic injustice.

What else stood out to you about this essential understanding from Jemar's teaching in the video and from this chapter in *How to Fight Racism*?

_____

_____

_____

_____

_____

_____

_____

How does this understanding change your view of the world around you?

_____

_____

_____

_____

2. It's about Impact, Not Intent

In many professional organizations and in politics, the difficulty of proving intent means that almost nothing is ever deemed racist. Even overt racists know enough to conceal their beliefs and can easily claim they weren't being racist if evidence of intent is found. So instead of focusing on intent, more attention should be paid to the impact or outcome of an action. Intent matters, but impact is what is critical in evaluating the fairness of a rule or practice. We must look to outcomes to evaluate whether or not a policy has impact, moving us closer to or further from justice.

What else stood out to you about this essential understanding from Jemar's teaching in the video and from this chapter in *How to Fight Racism*?

_____

_____

_____

_____

_____

_____

How does this understanding change your view of the world around you?

_____

_____

_____

_____

3. What Is Worth Conserving?

When it comes to political policies as they relate to race, this is the crucial question we must be asking. From the earliest days of the United States, racism and white supremacy have been codified in official laws and policies. When racial inequality gets inscribed in policy, those policies must change.

What else stood out to you about this essential understanding from Jemar's teaching in the video and from this chapter in *How to Fight Racism*?

_____

_____

_____

_____

_____

_____

_____

_____

_____

How does this understanding change your view of the world around you?

_____

_____

_____

_____

Taking Action: Racial Justice Practices

Now reflect on the racial justice practices Jemar provided in the video teaching, as well as the additional content for each of these practices found in chapter 9 of *How to Fight Racism*. You may want to review the notes you took during the teaching session regarding each racial justice practice as you read the corresponding questions.

1. Advocate for Voting Rights

Despite our long history of civil-rights activism, the democratic principle of "one person, one vote" remains in peril today. Even with automatic voter registration and mail-in voting options, exercising the right to vote has become increasingly difficult, especially for racial and ethnic minorities. Voting is a civically sacred right and duty, and yet so many people of color have been subject to voting disenfranchisement at some point in history. Part of fighting racism includes a commitment to protect the right of racial and ethnic minorities to vote. Here are ways you can help:

- *Look up the voting laws in your state.*
- *Pay special attention to any laws enacted after the 2013 Shelby v. Holder decision.*
- *Advocate for the restoration of the preclearance provision of the Voting Rights Act.*
- *Promote laws to restore voting rights to the formerly incarcerated.*
- *Become an election observer and report any measures that make it harder for people to vote.*
- *Ensure that people who are eligible to vote are registered through voter registration rallies and drives.*
- *Help people on election days by providing transportation, information, and other support to ensure voters get to the polls.*

What else stood out to you about this racial justice practice from Jemar's teaching in the video and from this chapter in *How to Fight Racism*?

_____
_____
_____
_____
_____
_____
_____

How does this understanding change your view of the world around you?

_____
_____
_____
_____

2. Work on Immigration Reform

In 2018, the Trump administration passed a "zero tolerance" policy for all people who attempted to enter the US unlawfully. This policy means that adults who had children with them as they attempted to enter the US were separated from their children, a practice commonly known as "family separation." Even if their parents came to the country unlawfully, young people who did not have a choice in the matter should have a way to stay in the country without fear of deportation. Other immigration reforms include:

- *Creating a pathway to citizenship that would allow current undocumented immigrants to engage in a process to become documented citizens.*
- *Proposing to extend healthcare to undocumented immigrants, close detention centers, and abolish the Immigrations and Customs Enforcement (ICE) department.*
- *Making your opinions known to state and federal officials through phone calls, messages, and letters.*
- *Donating to organizations like the Immigrant Justice Corps or World Relief to help with legal representation, awareness initiatives, and direct assistance to immigrants.*

What else stood out to you about this racial justice practice from Jemar's teaching in the video and from this chapter in *How to Fight Racism*?

_____

_____

_____

_____

_____

_____

_____

_____

_____

How does this understanding change your view of the world around you?

_____

_____

_____

_____

3. Pay Reparations

To this day, Black people still struggle to overcome the financial effects of the enslavement of their ancestors. Slavery at its most basic level was an economically exploitative system that boosted the profits of plantation owners by depriving enslaved African laborers of wages. Reparations, which simply means "repair," is one way to address the wealth gap due to racism. But reparations are not simply about what happened during slavery; they are about the debt owed to Black people for the economic disadvantages created by white supremacy before, during, and since the practice of race-based chattel slavery. Any serious racial justice efforts must consider the financial effects of racism by:

- *Bringing attention to this issue.*
- *Supporting the reparations study committee.*
- *Calling and writing letters to senators and representatives in support of reparations.*
- *Voting for candidates who support reparations.*
- *Discovering ways individuals and organizations can pay for reparations.*

What else stood out to you about this racial justice practice from Jemar's teaching in the video and from this chapter in *How to Fight Racism*?

_____
_____
_____
_____
_____
_____
_____
_____
_____
_____
_____

How will you put this practice into action in your own life?

_____
_____
_____
_____

4. Criminal Justice Reform

It is easy to assume that if people are guilty of a crime, then they deserve whatever punishments they receive behind bars. But it is important to remember that the process of ending up in prison is flawed and unfair at times. Extreme racial disparities exist that directly affect who gets put in prison. Despite making up just 13 percent of the overall US population, Black people represent 38 percent of the incarcerated population. In order to fight against racism on a systemic level, the criminal justice system must be reformed. Here's where we can start:

- *Abolish the death penalty.*
- *Eliminate cash bail.*
- *Reform or eliminate solitary confinement.*
- *Overhaul police practices.*

What else stood out to you about this racial justice practice from Jemar's teaching in the video and from this chapter in *How to Fight Racism*?

_____
_____
_____
_____
_____
_____
_____
_____

How will you put this practice into action in your own life?

_____
_____
_____

5. Promote Equitable Funding for Public Schools

People with resources and racial privilege have sought, in numerous ways, to keep their schools separate from "those kids"—meaning the poor and working-class students as well as families of color. This has resulted in vastly unequal funding and educational outcomes between white students and students of color. This disparity is often referred to as the "achievement gap," but some have contended that it is more appropriately termed the "opportunity gap" since students of color have not been afforded the same opportunities as their white counterparts. People committed to racial justice must see this opportunity gap as a central concern.

What else stood out to you about this racial justice practice from Jemar's teaching in the video and from this chapter in *How to Fight Racism*?

_____
_____
_____
_____
_____
_____
_____

How will you put this practice into action in your own life?

_____
_____
_____
_____

Be Specific: Your Next Step

What specific step will you take this week as a result of what you've learned and explored today? Pay attention to the areas where you felt most convicted as you moved through this material.

Consider this: If you're struggling to think of something on your own, *pick one specific racial justice practice that struck a deep chord with you and do one of the suggested actions listed in the practice.*

As a result of what I learned in this session, I will:

_____
_____
_____
_____
_____

And I will do this by:

_____ (date)

Pray

Take a few moments to reflect on what you've learned today and over the course of session 9. Invite God into your commitment to the fight against racism and the journey toward racial justice. Ask God to give you clarity regarding which specific action steps to take with the practices listed in this session. Ask God to give you the courage to continue to love in public with these practices. Thank God for his promise to always be with you—in your courage and your fear. Use this space to write out your prayer or journal your thoughts.

_____
_____
_____
_____
_____
_____
_____
_____
_____
_____

For Next Week: Read chapter 10 in *How to Fight Racism* and use the space below to write any insights or questions from your personal study that you want to discuss at the next group meeting.

_____
_____
_____
_____
_____
_____
_____
_____
_____
_____

Journal, Reflections, and Notes

HOW TO ORIENT YOUR LIFE TO RACIAL JUSTICE

*If we could change ourselves, the tendencies in the world
would also change. As a man changes his own nature,
so does the attitude of the world change towards him. . . .
We need not wait to see what others do.*

—MAHATMA GANDHI

Welcome

Welcome to session 10 of *How to Fight Racism*. Orienting your life toward racial justice requires constant reflection and action. It is not a one-time decision. We all have the responsibility daily to decide to take another step on the journey toward racial justice. Fighting racism is ultimately about serving other people from a wellspring of love. A spirit of loving service has to be infused with a spirit of humility that puts the interest of others before our own. The ARC of Racial Justice is demonstrated not in the times when everyone is talking about race but in those times when it would be easy or expected to overlook race. Every day, people of color in the United States are reminded that they are different or "other." They are reminded of their marginalized status when they try to hail a cab or use a ride share service, when someone tries to pronounce their name, when they are zoned for a particular school, when they receive a paycheck with a lower amount than their white peer, when they see another instance of police brutality enacted against them. By contrast, white people rarely have to think about themselves in racial terms. So for white people, remaining conscious of race and orienting their lives toward racial justice, even when they have the option of not doing so, demonstrates genuine solidarity with people of color. Today we will discuss a few crucial practices that will help you orient your entire life around racial justice. These practices will hone your racial reflexes so you can respond nimbly and adeptly to the various ways you will continue to encounter justice, and because fighting racism does not consist of a set of isolated actions that you take, these actions must flow from a disposition that is oriented toward racial justice. We have to reposition ourselves spiritually, emotionally, culturally, intellectually, and politically to address the myriad ways that racism manifests in the present day. Orienting your life in this way is about helping to make society more equitable and just for the generations that follow.

Share

Take a few minutes to discuss one of the following statements:

- How do you remain conscious of race even when you're in situations or circumstances where you don't have to?
   —or—
- What does it mean to orient your life toward racial justice?

Watch

Play the video segment for session 10. As you watch, use the following outline to record any thoughts or concepts that stand out to you.

Notes

Racial Justice is about the attitude, disposition, and orientation of one's entire life.

Orienting or Reorienting Our Lives toward the Good of Our Neighbor

What is wrong with the world?
—THE TIMES, LONDON

Dear sirs, I am.
—G. K. CHESTERTON

Principal: We are all caught in the problem of racism. We all have a responsibility to work toward solutions.

> **Do nothing out of selfish ambition or vain conceit.**
> **Rather, in humility value others above yourselves.**
> —PHILIPPIANS 2:3

Essential Understandings
1. Humility

2. We Have to Keep the Light Switch On
A light switch vs. a smoke alarm
White friends, don't go back to "business as usual."

Racial Justice Practices
1. Budgeting Our Time
Practicing racial justice takes time.
- Look at the organizations or causes you want to be a part of.
- Estimate how much time it will take to contribute in these places on a consistent basis (weekly or monthly).
- Rearrange things to make time for it.

2. Budgeting Our Money
Tithing means giving away a tenth of one's earnings.
- Think about the organizations and causes you want to support—especially Black and minority-led institutions.
- Think about how *much* you can give rather than how *little* you can give.
- Give sacrificially.

3. Be Careful about Referencing Racists

> **Would you quote Columbus to Cherokees?**
> **Would you quote Cortez to Aztecs, even if they theology was good?**
> **It just sings a blind privilege, wouldn't you agree?**
> **Your precious Puritans.**
> —JASON "PROPAGANDA" PETTY,
> "PRECIOUS PURITANS" (2012)

There is a *difference* between teaching about these historical figures for educational purposes and teaching them as admirable figures to emulate.

- Tell the whole story.
- Inform yourself about the people whom you are referencing.
- Choose different historical figures to reference.
- Be careful about who we place on a pedestal.

Refuse to platform racists.

> *We need to put creative, constructive*
> *pressure on people to change their views*
> *for the sake of racial justice.*
> —JEMAR TISBY

4. Consider Taking Your Business to a Minority-Led Institution
We have an abundance of talents and skills to offer.

5. Reconsider Where We Send Our Kids to School
This is about cultivating an attitude toward the common good.

> *True integration, true equality requires*
> *a surrendering of advantage. And*
> *when it comes to our own children,*
> *that can feel almost unnatural.*
> —NIKOLE HANNAH-JONES

What are we going to do in our own families to address the inequality we see in schools?

Write a new story of justice and equity in our public schools.

List of Questions to Ask to Ensure Racial Equity
- *How and where does the curriculum specifically address Black history, Native American history, and the histories of other people of color?*
- *What training do teachers receive in order to provide culturally responsive pedagogy?*
- *Are there written protocols and guidelines addressing hate speech and racist incidents at school?*

- *Do you track disciplines, suspensions, and expulsions by race and ethnicity?*
- *How do those data compare across demographics?*

The idea: accountability for organizations and institutions to practices that promote racial justice and equity

Orienting your life toward racial justice requires constant focus, continual attention, and a daily decision.

We *all* have the responsibility to take steps toward racial justice.

Discuss

Take a few minutes with your group members to discuss what you just watched and explore these concepts in Scripture.

1. What stood out to you from Jemar's teaching on how to orient your life to racial justice?

_____

_____

_____

_____

2. How have you started to orient your life toward racial justice as a result of participating in this study over the past few weeks?

_____

_____

_____

_____

3. How do you plan to "keep the light switch on" in the fight against racism in your own life and in the life of your community? How will you encourage others to do the same?

_____

_____

_____

_____

4. Which racial justice practice resonates the most with you? Most often this will be the practice we feel convicted by or motivated to start practicing right away.

_____

_____

_____

5. What changes will you make to start budgeting your time and your money toward racial justice?

_____

_____

_____

6. How will you be mindful of referencing racists in your language, your examples, and your social media posts? Where will you go to find different sources of educational and historical figures?

_____

_____

_____

7. How can you contribute your talents to minority-led institutions?

_____

_____

_____

8. Do you need to reconsider where your kids go to school? If so, process this with your group. If you don't have kids in school or kids in your care, how can you contribute to the overall equity and racial justice of your school district? Who can you meet with or where will you go to ask the questions provided by Jemar?

_____

_____

_____

_____

_____

_____

_____

Pray

Pray as a group before you close your time together. Ask God to show you how you can orient your life toward racial justice in a way that has the greatest impact on you and your community. Use this space to keep track of prayer requests and group updates.

_____

_____

_____

_____

_____

_____

_____

_____

_____

_____

_____

_____

_____

_____

_____

_____

_____

_____

_____

_____

_____

_____

_____

_____

_____

_____

_____

_____

BETWEEN-SESSIONS PERSONAL STUDY

Weekly Reflection

Before you begin the between-sessions exercises, briefly review your video notes for session 10. In the space below, write down the *most significant point* you took away from this session.

_____

_____

_____

_____

Diving Deeper: Essential Understandings

Reflect on the essential understandings Jemar provided in the video teaching, as well as the additional content for each of these essential understandings found in chapter 10 of *How to Fight Racism*. You may want to review the notes you took during the teaching session regarding each essential understanding as you read the corresponding questions.

1. Cancel Contempt

Feelings of contempt dehumanize other people and cause us to replicate the hate we wish to eradicate. We must constantly check our hearts to ensure that we are not demonstrating contempt for others. The temptation to look down on others because of their backward views on race and diversity easily descends into disdain and haughtiness. A distorted understanding of personhood leads to feelings of superiority or inferiority. Contempt is the poison pill of racial justice.

What else stood out to you about this essential understanding from Jemar's teaching in the video and from this chapter in *How to Fight Racism*?

_____

_____

_____

_____

_____

_____

_____

How does this understanding change your view of the world around you?

_____

_____

_____

_____

2. Humility: Have This Mind among Yourselves

To pursue racial justice we must cultivate humility—to listen and learn, yes, but also to admit that we, too, can act in racist ways. White people must recognize with humility that, although life can be difficult for anyone, their skin color has not added to their hardships. And people of color must recognize that, despite their life experiences, they can sometimes get it wrong when it comes to race. Anyone can get it wrong, especially when it comes to racial justice. The key is having humility, owning your mistakes, learning from them, and staying on the journey.

What else stood out to you about this essential understanding from Jemar's teaching in the video and from this chapter in *How to Fight Racism*?

_____

_____

_____

_____

_____

_____

How does this understanding change your view of the world around you?

_____

_____

_____

_____

3. Keep the Light Switch On

There's a big difference between a light switch and a smoke alarm. A light switch can be turned on and off. A smoke alarm is always on. Racial justice for white people is like a light switch. You can turn it on or off whenever you feel like it. But for people of color, racial justice is more like a smoke alarm. It always has to be on just to keep safe and avoid danger. It is important to remain conscious of race even when you have the option of not doing so. And you can keep the racial justice light switch on by setting up structures and routines that make this possible. Here are a few suggestions for keeping the light switch on:

- *Participate in groups that make race a constant topic—book studies, activist organizations, nonprofits, etc.*
- *Attend a church that makes racial justice a core commitment.*
- *Make meaningful friendships and professional relationships with people of color or people different than you.*

What else stood out to you about this essential understanding from Jemar's teaching in the video and from this chapter in *How to Fight Racism*?

_____

_____

_____

_____

_____

_____

_____

How does this understanding change your view of the world around you?

_____

_____

_____

_____

Taking Action: Racial Justice Practices

Now reflect on the racial justice practices Jemar provided in the video teaching, as well as the additional content for each of these practices found in chapter 10 of *How to Fight Racism*. You may want to review the notes you took during the teaching session regarding each racial justice practice as you read the corresponding questions.

1. Budget Your Time toward Racial Justice

To practice racial justice, you must make the time for it. And getting serious about fighting racism entails auditing how you spend your time so you can make room for justice concerns. Remember, the journey toward racial justice consists not simply in external action but in internal reflection as well. The time you spend thinking, praying, and processing is time that counts toward fighting racism too.

What else stood out to you about this racial justice practice from Jemar's teaching in the video and from this chapter in *How to Fight Racism*?

_____

_____

_____

_____

_____

_____

_____

_____

How does this understanding change your view of the world around you?

_____

_____

_____

_____

2. Give Sacrificially

Not everyone has the luxury of a salary large enough to give away most of their income and still support themselves, but the principle of generous, sacrificial giving is universal. Even the tithing concept of the Bible, which still stands true, was meant to support the marginalized and oppressed. Consider how you can engage in racial justice practices by giving at the organizational level and the individual level. And don't fall victim to the "golden handcuffs," the idea that one can be so tied to making money and living a materially comfortable life that it becomes a prison preventing you from doing what may be less lucrative but is more beneficial for you and others.

What else stood out to you about this racial justice practice from Jemar's teaching in the video and from this chapter in *How to Fight Racism*?

_____

_____

_____

_____

_____

_____

_____

_____

How does this understanding change your view of the world around you?

_____

_____

_____

_____

3. Be Careful about Referencing Racists

Don't overlook the racism of the people you might reference. We cannot change the record of leaders and historical figures who held abhorrent racial views. And if we want to talk about the political foundations of the United States, it's impossible not to mention someone with racist views—even George Washington owned slaves. But what we can do is make sure these parts of their record are known just as much as the admirable parts. We can discuss the impact of their actions on people who held less power, had less money, and were part of groups considered minorities, subhuman, or "other." You can bring attention to this issue by:

- *Speaking directly and honestly about a person's racial record—even if it's uncomfortable.*
- *Not citing racists at all.*

- *Researching and sharing about people who fought racism and other forms of injustice and use them as examples.*
- *Refusing to platform racists. This might look like refusing to repost them on social media, refusing to buy their products, or refusing to listen to their speeches to discourage racist behavior.*
- *Using your platform productively. This might look like the short list of Black athletes who used their prominence as celebrities to advance the cause of racial justice. Here's how to do this productively: determine your platform, be public about it, say the right things in the right way, and prepare for the reaction.*

What else stood out to you about this racial justice practice from Jemar's teaching in the video and from this chapter in *How to Fight Racism*?

_____

_____

_____

_____

_____

_____

_____

_____

_____

_____

How will you put this practice into action in your own life?

_____

_____

_____

_____

4. Support Minority-Owned or -Led Businesses

Racial and ethnic minorities should consider the difficulties that many minority-owned or -led organizations have in recruiting their top-tier talent and securing financial resources for their mission. If more people of color chose to attend school or work for these institutions, it could breathe new life into their work. That is why Black people and other people of color are encouraged to practice racial justice with yet another action step by **taking their skills, talents, and expertise to minority-owned or -led organizations.**

What else stood out to you about this racial justice practice from Jemar's teaching in the video and from this chapter in *How to Fight Racism*?

_____

_____

_____

_____

_____

_____

How will you put this practice into action in your own life?

_____

_____

_____

_____

5. Support Candidates Committed to Racial Justice—or Run Yourself

At some point we need to get involved in making the changes we say need to happen. Orienting your life toward racial justice must entail ongoing involvement at the policy level. While you may never actually run for elected office, all political campaigns depend on volunteers for success. And if you're thinking of running for elected office, remember the opportunities for public policy work span from the national to the local level—from school board to city council, district attorney to county commissioner, sheriff to judge, state representative to city clerk. If you're considering running for office, be advised to:

- *Consult with experts and advisers.*
- *Listen to your potential constituents to form a platform.*
- *Seek input from people with fundraising and campaign managing experience.*

What else stood out to you about this racial justice practice from Jemar's teaching in the video and from this chapter in *How to Fight Racism*?

_____

_____

_____

_____

_____

_____

How will you put this practice into action in your own life?

_____

_____

_____

_____

6. Reconsider Where You Send Your Kids to School

Every parent of school-age children must face the choice of where to send their children to school and what that means for racial segregation in schools. As long as people who can afford the financial and cultural costs of segregation choose to send their children to separate schools, vast inequality will remain in the system. Parents must seriously consider the value of racial integration in comparison with better material resources at other schools. It may be that your racial justice journey includes taking the bold step of sending your children to a less prestigious school in order to help write a new story about integration and achievement in our public schools.

What else stood out to you about this racial justice practice from Jemar's teaching in the video and from this chapter in _How to Fight Racism_?

_____

_____

_____

_____

_____

_____

How will you put this practice into action in your own life?

_____

_____

_____

7. Ensure Local Schools Practice Racial Justice

Regardless of where you send your kids to school or even if you have kids at all, you can ensure that your local schools are building racial justice into their curriculum. Here's how—ask the following questions that can also be modified for any school, club, sports team, nonprofit, or other organizations:

- *How and where does the curriculum specifically address Black history, Native American history, and the histories of other people of color?*
- *What training do teachers receive on culturally responsive teaching and working with racial and ethnic minority students and families?*
- *Are there written protocols and guidelines addressing hate speech and racist incidents (including cyberbullying) at school?*
- *What is the racial/ethnic composition of the school board, faculty, staff, and support staff (i.e., anyone on the payroll)?*
- *What is the retention rate/tenure of racial and ethnic minority faculty and staff compared to their white peers?*
- *Have you considered hiring racial and ethnic minorities in clusters instead of one or two at a time?*
- *Do you track discipline, suspensions, and expulsions by race and ethnicity? How do those data compare across demographics?*
- *Have you had focus groups where parents and guardians of color get a chance to speak into school practices and climate?*
- *What have you learned from other schools or institutions about the best practices for racial justice? Have you considered forming a standing committee on racial awareness and responsiveness so you can be proactive about racial justice and not always reactive?*

What else stood out to you about this racial justice practice from Jemar's teaching in the video and from this chapter in *How to Fight Racism*?

_____

_____

_____

_____

_____

_____

_____

_____

_____

How will you put this practice into action in your own life?

_____

_____

_____

_____

Be Specific: Your Next Step

What specific step will you take this week as a result of what you've learned and explored today? Pay attention to the areas where you felt most convicted as you moved through this material.

Consider this: If you're struggling to think of something on your own, *consider the references you use most often in life—from books, movies, historical figures. Do your research to see if they have a racist past. If so, find new references to use and keep track of the significance of their stories so you can teach people about your new references too.*

As a result of what I learned in this session, I will:

_____

_____

_____

_____

_____

_____

_____

_____

_____

And I will do this by:
_____ (date)

Pray

Take a few moments to reflect on what you've learned today and over the course of session 9. Invite God into your commitment to the fight against racism and the journey toward racial justice. Ask God to give you clarity regarding which specific action steps to take regarding the practices listed in this session. Ask God to give you the courage to continue to love in public with these practices. Thank God for his promise to always be with you—in your courage and your fear. Use this space to write out your prayer or journal your thoughts.

_____

_____

_____

_____

_____

_____

_____

Journal, Reflections, and Notes

_____

_____

_____

_____

_____

_____

_____

_____

_____

_____

_____

_____

_____

_____

_____

_____

_____

_____

_____

_____

_____

_____

_____

_____

_____

_____

_____

CONCLUSION

*This struggle against racism and this journey toward racial justice
isn't just about how it changes the world, but how it changes you.*
—JEMAR TISBY

Welcome to the conclusion of *How to Fight Racism*. Assuming your group meets one more time to discuss the conclusion of this study, remember this: *fighting racism is not just about how it changes the world; it's also about how it changes you.* May this journey of courageous Christianity and this journey toward the full ARC of Racial Justice bring you to a deeper sense of three important realities: *God's presence, the community of co-laborers,* and *your own identity.* God will not always make our lives easier when we take on the cause of racial justice, but God will make himself known to us. And while this journey may alienate us from some, it will draw us closer into community with many others who are on the journey too. Fighting racial justice will also teach you more about *you*—your own fragility, your own preconceived notions and judgmentalism, your own resilience and strength. To those who worry about what it might cost to take bolder steps down this journey of racial justice: *the only way to grow is to go.* So get started. The steps do not have to be hard, but if you keep going, baby steps turn into long strides toward freedom. And to those who are tired from the journey but keep trudging along, know this: *you are already effective.* You have already succeeded because you got started. You are one of the few who chose to take on the risks of fighting racism and in that decision, you have already achieved victory. Each day that we live is an opportunity to be witnesses to the resurrection life and the coming of the kingdom of God. We pray *and work* for that kingdom to come and for God's will to be done right here and now so that we might be courageous Christians on the journey toward racial justice.

Share

Take a few minutes to discuss one of the following statements:

- How has the journey toward racial justice changed you?
  —or—
- In what new ways will you engage in the fight against racism as a result of what you learned in this study?

Watch

Play the four-minute video segment for the conclusion. As you watch, use the following outline to record any thoughts or concepts that stand out to you.

Notes
Fannie Lou Hamer

> *This struggle against racism and this journey toward racial justice isn't just about how it changes the world but how it changes you.*
> **—JEMAR TISBY**

The Three Realities of the Racial Justice Journey
1. God's Presence

When the fight against racism is the hardest, that's when we feel God's presence most closely.

2. The Community of Co-Laborers

We are not alone on this journey.

3. Myself

Beyond the fear and exhaustion, there are deep reservoirs of strength.

> *It's a funny thing, ever since I started working for Christ, it's like the 23rd Psalm. "Thou anointeth my head and you prepare a table for me in the presence of my enemies."*
> **—FANNIE LOU HAMER**

To the fearful:
- The only way to grow is to go.
- Get started.
- Take small steps and persevere.

To those who have already been on this journey:
- You have already been effective.
- You are already victorious.
- You are already faithful.

> *Hope is not blind optimism. Hope is a realistic*
> *assessment of things as they are with the*
> *faith that things can be different.*
> —JEMAR TISBY

Today is the day to fight racism and join the journey toward racial justice.

Discuss

1. How have you experienced a greater sense of awareness and understanding of God as you've embarked on this journey of how to fight racism?

   _____

   _____

   _____

   _____

   _____

   _____

2. How have you experienced a greater sense of awareness and understanding of the community of co-laborers around you on this journey?

   _____

   _____

   _____

   _____

   _____

   _____

3. How have you witnessed or experienced the "deep reservoirs of strength" in those around you? Share specific examples of individuals who come to mind.

_____

_____

_____

_____

4. At the end of this session, Jemar gives a word of encouragement to the "trepidatious" who are about to start the journey toward racial justice and to those who are already on the journey. Where are you, and why?

_____

_____

_____

_____

5. Which one of his encouragements sticks with you, and why?

_____

_____

_____

6. What is your single biggest "aha" moment or takeaway from this study?

_____

_____

_____

_____

7. What specific actions will you take to start or continue on the journey of racial justice this week? How can your group hold you accountable to these actions?

_____

_____

_____

_____

_____

_____

Pray

Pray as a group before you close your time together. Ask God to show you how this journey toward racial justice has changed you. Invite God into your journey of living as a courageous Christian who cares about moving toward racial justice in the world around you. Use this space to keep track of prayer requests and group updates.

_____

_____

_____

_____

_____

_____

_____

_____

_____

_____

_____

_____

_____

_____

_____

_____

_____

_____

_____

_____

_____

_____

_____

_____

_____

_____

_____

CLOSING WORDS

When I began intentionally dedicating my time, expertise, and energy to fighting racism, my life did not become easier. In many ways, it became harder. I opened myself up to arguments and attacks. Relationships became strained and some were broken. In many ways, I became like the "man of sorrows" described by Isaiah the prophet (Isa. 53:3 ESV). And I'm guessing the same may be true for some of you. Maybe this has *been* your journey, and maybe for others it will *become* your journey. Either way, hang in there. We cannot give up. As Christians, we are meant to be a people of hope because we believe that a poor carpenter from Nazareth conquered death and is forming a people who will join in this triumph.

The ARC of Racial Justice encourages us to build our awareness, deepen our relationships, and strengthen our commitments—not just in our society but also inside our own souls. By taking steps to reflect on our experiences with race individually and systemically, we can better understand our attitudes on the topic and take the necessary steps on the journey of racial justice, coming alongside like-minded, justice-oriented, loving people who share this goal.

The journey for racial justice continues. And the music we hear along the way is not a funeral dirge; it is festival music leading us to a banquet of blessings and a harvest of righteousness. Today is the day and now is the time to join this journey toward racial justice.

Grace and peace,
Jemar Tisby

LEADER'S GUIDE

Group Size

The *How to Fight Racism* video study is designed to be experienced in a group setting such as a Bible study, Sunday school class, or any small group gathering. To ensure everyone has enough time to participate in discussions, it is recommended that large groups break up into smaller groups of four to six people each.

Materials Needed

Each participant should have her own study guide, which includes notes for video segments, directions for activities and discussion questions, and personal studies to deepen learning between sessions.

Timing

Each session will take between two and three hours. For those who have less time available to meet, you can use fewer questions for discussion. You may also opt to devote two meetings to each session.

Facilitation

Each group should appoint a facilitator who is responsible for starting the video and for keeping track of time during discussions and activities. Facilitators may also read questions aloud and monitor discussions, prompting participants to respond and assuring that everyone has the opportunity to participate.

Personal Studies

Maximize the impact of the curriculum with additional study between group sessions. There are personal studies available for each session. Feel free to engage with these optional study materials as much or as little as you need.

How to Fight Racism

Courageous Christianity and the Journey Toward Racial Justice

Jemar Tisby

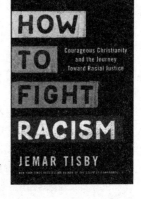

Racism is pervasive in today's world, and many are complicit in the failure to confront its evils. Jemar Tisby, author of the *New York Times* bestseller *The Color of Compromise*, believes we need to move beyond mere discussions about racism and begin equipping people with the practical tools to fight against it.

What you'll learn:

- Framework for action
  - Discover an array of actionable items to confront racism in relationships and everyday life through a simple framework—the ARC of Racial Justice—that helps readers consistently interrogate their own actions and maintain a consistent posture of antiracist action.
- More productive conversations
  - Reject passivity and become an active participant in the struggle for human dignity across racial and ethnic lines. Discover a clear model for how to think about race in productive ways, and a compelling call to dismantle a social hierarchy long stratified by skin color.
- Principles for the church
  - Activate an opportunity for the local church to be part of the solution, and begin to apply principles that offer hope that will transform our nation and the world.

Available in stores and online!

How to Fight Racism Video Study

Courageous Christianity and the Journey Toward Racial Justice

Jemar Tisby

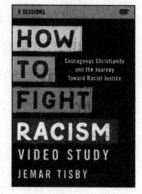

How to Fight Racism Video Study is a how-to guide for pursuing racial justice. It is long past time to move beyond mere discussions about racism. People need practical tools and suggestions to actually do something about it.

By providing a series of hands-on suggestions for practice bolstered by real-world examples of change, Jemar Tisby offers viewers an array of actionable items to help them become proactive initiators of racial justice. Far more than a simple list of items to do, it also provides a simple framework to help viewers consistently interrogate their own actions and maintain a posture of antiracist action. This video study is for anyone who believes it is time for the church to stop compromising with racism and courageously confront it.

How to Fight Racism Video Study offers viewers the opportunity to be part of the solution to racial problems in the church and the nation. It equips them to become activists in the cause of racial justice and to see themselves as participants in the struggle for human dignity across racial and ethnic lines. In the end, viewers of the study will have a model for how to think about race in productive ways and to lend their energy in dismantling a social hierarchy that has long been stratified by skin color.

Available in stores and online!

The Color of Compromise

The Truth about the American Church's Complicity in Racism

Jemar Tisby

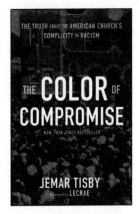

The Color of Compromise is both enlightening and compelling, telling a history we either ignore or just don't know. Equal parts painful and inspirational, it details how the American church has helped create and maintain racist ideas and practices. You will be guided in thinking through concrete solutions for improved race relations and a racially inclusive church.

The Color of Compromise:

- Takes you on a historical, sociological, and religious journey from America's early colonial days through slavery and the Civil War
- Covers the tragedy of Jim Crow laws, the victories of the Civil Rights era, and the strides of today's Black Lives Matter movement
- Reveals the cultural and institutional tables we have to flip in order to bring about meaningful integration
- Charts a path forward to replace established patterns and systems of complicity with bold, courageous, immediate action
- Is a perfect book for pastors and other faith leaders, students, nonstudents, book clubs, small group studies, history lovers, and all lifelong learners

The Color of Compromise is not a call to shame or a platform to blame white evangelical Christians. It is a call from a place of love and desire to fight for a more racially unified church that no longer compromises what the Bible teaches about human dignity and equality. A call that challenges black and white Christians alike to standup now and begin implementing the concrete ways Tisby outlines, all for a more equitable and inclusive environment among God's people. Starting today.

Available in stores and online!

JESUS
IN ME

Experiencing *the* Holy Spirit
as a Constant Companion

STUDY GUIDE + STREAMING VIDEO
EIGHT SESSIONS

ANNE
GRAHAM
LOTZ

HarperChristian
Resources

Jesus in Me Study Guide
Copyright © 2020, 2022 by Anne Graham Lotz

Requests for information should be addressed to:
HarperChristian Resources, 3900 Sparks Dr. SE, Grand Rapids, Michigan 49546

ISBN 978-0-310-14675-9 (softcover)
ISBN 978-0-310-14676-6 (ebook)

Quotations by Anne Graham Lotz throughout the study guide are from the book *Jesus in Me* (Colorado Springs: Multnomah, 2019).

Published in association with the literary agency of Alive Communications, Inc., 7680 Goddard Street, Suite 200, Colorado Springs, CO 80920. www.alivecommunications.com

Cover design: Kristopher K. Orr
Interior design: Kathryn Murray

First Printing May 2022 / Printed in the United States of America

JESUS
IN ME

CONTENTS

ABOUT ANNE GRAHAM LOTZ   vii

PREFACE   ix

ABOUT THE STUDY   xi

SESSION 1: BIBLE STUDY WORKSHOP   1

SESSION 2: LOVING THE *Person* OF THE HOLY SPIRIT   11

SESSION 3: ENJOYING THE *Presence* OF THE HOLY SPIRIT   31

SESSION 4: RELYING ON THE *Power* OF THE HOLY SPIRIT   51

SESSION 5: EMBRACING THE *Purpose* OF THE HOLY SPIRIT   71

SESSION 6: LIVING BY THE *Precepts* OF THE HOLY SPIRIT   91

SESSION 7: REFLECTING THE *Purity* OF THE HOLY SPIRIT   111

SESSION 8: TRUSTING IN THE *Priority* OF THE HOLY SPIRIT   131

FACILITATOR'S GUIDE   151

ABOUT
ANNE GRAHAM LOTZ

CALLED "THE BEST PREACHER IN THE FAMILY" by her father, Billy Graham, Anne Graham Lotz speaks around the globe with the wisdom and authority of years spent studying God's Word.

The *New York Times* named Anne one of the five most influential evangelists of her generation. She's been profiled on *60 Minutes* and has appeared on TV programs such as *Larry King Live, The Today Show,* and *Hannity Live*. Her Just Give Me Jesus revivals have been held in more than thirty cities in twelve different countries, to hundreds of thousands of attendees.

Whether a delegate to Davos' Economic Forum, a commentator to the *Washington Post*, or a groundbreaking speaker on platforms throughout the world, Anne's aim is clear—to bring revival to the hearts of God's people. And her message is consistent—calling people into a personal relationship with God through His Word and through prayer.

In May 2016, Anne was named the Chairperson of the National Day of Prayer Task Force, a position held by only two other women, Shirley Dobson and Vonette Bright, since its inception in 1952.

Anne is a bestselling and award-winning author. Her most recent releases are *The Light of His Presence, Jesus in Me, The Daniel Prayer, Wounded by God's People, Fixing My Eyes on Jesus, Expecting to See Jesus,* and her first children's book, *Heaven: God's Promise for Me*.

Anne and her late husband, Danny Lotz, have three grown children and three grandchildren. She is the founder and president of AnGeL Ministries, an independent, non-profit organization based in Raleigh, North Carolina, that is committed to giving out messages of biblical exposition so God's Word is personal and relevant to ordinary people.

The ministry's name is derived from the initials of Anne Graham Lotz (AGL) and is especially fitting, as angels are messengers of God who go wherever He sends, speak to whomever He directs, and faithfully deliver His Word. AnGeL Ministries serves as the umbrella organization for the diverse ministry of Anne Graham Lotz—including her many books, DVDs, CDs, speaking engagements, and special events.

To learn more about Anne and AnGeL Ministries, visit
www.annegrahamlotz.org.

PREFACE

Recently I went to the ENT doctor because I thought I had reached the stage of needing hearing aids. The doctor tested me, then concluded, "Mrs. Lotz, you don't need hearing aids because you have virtually no hearing loss. Your problem is that you don't listen." I couldn't help but laugh because I knew he was right! When I'm tired or busy, I don't always pay attention to someone who is speaking. And if the person is fairly long-winded, my mind will wander to other things. As a result, I'm disconnected. Distracted. Even though I hear the sound of the voice, I don't know what's being said because I'm not listening.

The same thing is true when it comes to reading my Bible. I can read the words, yet not really hear what God is saying because I'm rushing through my reading, or distracted by wandering thoughts, or focused only on facts and information, or just too tired to concentrate. As a result, my daily time with Him in His Word becomes routine. Drudgery. A "have-to," not a "want-to" exercise.

Learning to listen for God's voice speaking to me through the pages of my Bible has transformed my daily time with Him. I now approach the time with eager anticipation of what He will say. Perhaps more than any other aspect of my Christian life, it has drawn me closer to Him in an intimate relationship. It has become the very core of who I am. Because, dear friend, God *does* speak through His Word. I *know* . . .!

This video Bible study, *Jesus in Me*, is designed to teach you how to listen to the whispers of the Holy Spirit as you read God's Word. It has been patterned after my own daily devotional exercise. I'm excited for you to discover the joy of hearing God's voice speaking to you personally as you learn to listen.

Every blessing,

Anne Graham Lotz

ABOUT THE STUDY

THIS STUDY GUIDE IS TO BE USED WITH the video-based course *Jesus in Me: Experiencing the Holy Spirit as a Constant Companion.* As an integral part of the course, it provides a format for Bible study that serves as the basis for both small group use (Sunday school classes, women's or men's groups, home or neighborhood studies, one-on-one discipleship) and individual use. This guide will lead you through a series of questions that will enable you to not only discover for yourself the eternal truths revealed by God in the Bible, but also to hear God speaking personally to you through His Word. You then will be prepared to participate in a meaningful time of study and discussion with members of your small group.

INDIVIDUAL STUDY

Each week you will work through 5 Bible studies on selected passages of Scripture using the 3-question steps you will learn during the workshop in session 1. Before you meet with your group, be sure to take the time to reflect and record your *Live in Obedient Response* statements to share with your group so they can encourage you and hold you accountable.

It is important to complete each individual study before your next session, as this will make the video presentation more meaningful to you during the small group time. Note that meaningful, daily Bible study will occur if you:

- Set aside a regular place for private devotions.
- Set aside a regular time for private devotions.
- Pray before beginning the day's assignment, asking God to speak to you through His Word.

- Write out your answers for each step, in sequence.
- Make the time to be still and listen, reflecting thoughtfully on your response in the final step.
- Don't rush—it may take time in prayerful meditation on a given passage to discover meaningful lessons and hear the Spirit's whispers.

Spiritual discipline is an essential part of your ability to grow in your relationship with God through knowledge and understanding of His Word. So, take your individual study seriously and allow God to speak to you from His Word.

GROUP STUDY

Note: Each session will require approximately 60 minutes of group meeting time to share the discoveries from Individual Bible study, watch the video, and discuss the teaching and content.

You will review the lessons, personal applications, and take-aways at the beginning of your group meeting and then watch the teaching from Anne. After each video teaching, there will be group discussion time to learn from one another and share in the experience of the Holy Spirit as a constant companion.

In session 1 of *Jesus In Me*, you will watch the video workshop and be introduced to the 3-question Bible study method. You will use John 14:15–20 during the workshop to help you better understand this approach. (Note that if your group meets less frequently than once a week, you may want to extend your study time for each passage.)

Space is provided for you to take notes during the video presentation. After the message, you will then have time to discuss the key concepts with your small group using the questions in this guide.

Note: If you are the facilitator for the group, there are additional instructions and resources provided in the back of this study guide. This guide will help you structure your meeting time, facilitate discussion times, and help you lead group members through the key points of the study.

INDIVIDUAL COMMITMENT

Remember that the real growth in this study will happen during your quiet times with God during the week. During the group times, you will have the opportunity to process what you have learned with the other members, ask questions, and learn from them as you listen to what God is doing in their lives. In addition, keep in mind that the videos, discussions, and activities in this study are simply meant to tune your heart and your spiritual ears to God's voice so that you can live out what He says as you grow closer to Him.

BIBLE STUDY WORKSHOP

This Bible study workshop has a single purpose: to present an approach that will help you learn to listen for God's voice, know Him in a personal relationship, and communicate with Him through His Word. The following information is introduced in detail in the video presentation. Use this section of the study guide as you view the workshop material. Underline key thoughts and take additional notes as you participate in the workshop. (Note that the passages Anne uses as examples in the video workshop are found on pages 6–7.)

WHAT YOU NEED

Before you begin the video workshop for this first session, you will need the following:

- ❑ this study guide + streaming video (access available on inside front cover) or DVD, sold separately
- ❑ a Bible
- ❑ pen or pencil
- ❑ time
- ❑ prayer
- ❑ an open heart

WATCH VIDEO SESSION 1 (49 MINUTES)

Anne will use this video session to walk you through the following 5 Steps to Bible study with the 3 questions that are essential to the Bible Study Workshop. She will illustrate how to do this Bible study with Colossians 1:26–27 (see pages 6–7 in your study guide).

STEPS TO BIBLE STUDY

STEP 1: READ GOD'S WORD
(Look at the Passage.)

The first step is to *read the Bible*. At the start of each session in this study guide, you will find the Scriptures listed in a column that you should read during the week. When you have finished reading the passage for the day, move on to Step 2.

STEP 2: WHAT DOES GOD'S WORD SAY?
(List the Facts.)

After reading the passage, make a verse-by-verse list of the outstanding facts. Don't get caught up in the details—just pinpoint the most obvious facts as they appear to you. When you make your list, do not paraphrase the text but use actual words from the passage. Look for the nouns and the verbs.

STEP 3: WHAT DOES GOD'S WORD MEAN?
(Learn the Lessons.)

After reading the passage and listing the facts, look for a lesson to learn from each fact. Ask yourself the following questions:

- *Who is speaking?*
- *What is the subject?*
- *Where is it taking place?*
- *When did it happen?*
- *What can I learn from what is taking place or what is being said?*

It may also help to ask yourself: *What are the people in the passage doing that I should be doing? Is there a command I should obey? A promise I should claim? A warning I should heed? An example I should follow?* Focus on spiritual lessons.

STEP 4: WHAT DOES GOD'S WORD MEAN IN MY LIFE?
(Listen to His Voice.)

Although this step will be the most meaningful for you, you can't do it effectively until you complete the first three steps. So, first rephrase the lessons you found in Step 3 and put them in the form of questions you could ask yourself, your spouse, your child, your friend, your neighbor, or your coworker. As you write the questions, listen for God to speak to you through His Word.

Be aware that there are some challenging passages in this study. Don't get hung up on what you don't understand, but just look for the *general principles* and *lessons* that can be learned. The introduction prior to the passages you will study in sessions 2–8, as well as the examples offered in Steps 2, 3, and 4 of this session, will help you get started.

Remember not to rush this process. It may take you several moments of prayerful meditation to discover meaningful lessons from the Scripture you are reading and hear God speaking to you. The object is not to "get through it" but to develop your personal relationship with God in order to grow in faith and learn to hear the whispers of the Holy Spirit.

STEP 5: LIVE IN OBEDIENT RESPONSE TO GOD'S WORD
(What will you do about what God has said?)

Read the assigned Scripture passages prayerfully, objectively, thoughtfully, and attentively as you listen for God to speak. Note that He may not speak to you through *every* verse, but He *will* speak. When He does, record the verse number (if applicable), what it is that God seems to be saying to you, and your response to Him. You might like to date these pages as a means not only of keeping a spiritual journal but also of holding yourself accountable to follow through in obedience. (See pages 6–7 for the example that Anne demonstrates in the video.) Afterward, it is your turn to try this method on your own using John 14:15–20. (See pages 8–9.)

STEP 1
Read God's Word
(Look at the Passage.)

Colossians 1:26–27

26 the mystery that has been kept hidden for ages and generations, but is now disclosed to the saints.

27 To them God has chosen to make known among the Gentiles the glorious riches of this mystery, which is Christ in you, the hope of glory.

STEP 2
What Does God's Word Say?
(List the Facts.)

- **Reread God's Word**
- **List the outstanding facts with verse numbers**
- **Do not paraphrase**

v. 26 the mystery kept hidden for ages

v. 26 but now disclosed

v. 27 God has chosen to make known this mystery

v. 27 which is Christ in you
v. 27 the hope of glory.

STEP 3
What Does God's Word Mean?
(Learn the Lessons.)

- **Write one spiritual lesson for each fact in Step 2.**
- **Is there an example to follow, a lesson to learn, a command to obey, a warning to heed, a promise to claim?**

v. 26 God does not always tell us everything. *The indwelling of the Holy Spirit was a mystery to Old Testament Saints.*

v. 26 There comes a time when God does reveal to us an understanding of the truth. *The indwelling of the Holy Spirit is no longer a mystery, but a truth to be understood.*

v. 27 Now is the time to grow in our understanding of that which we have not understood before.

v. 27 The mystery that Old Testament saints didn't know, and many people today do not understand, is that Jesus is available to dwell in us, in the Person of the Holy Spirit.

v. 27 Our confidence is that the Holy Spirit in us will conform us into the image of Jesus—that we will bring Him glory through our conduct and our character.

STEP 4
What Does God's Word Mean in My Life?
(Listen to His Voice.)

- **Put the lessons from Step 3 in the form of a question to ask yourself or someone else.**

v. 26 What have I not understood before now? Especially about the Holy Spirit?

v. 26 Is this the time when God will reveal to me a greater understanding of the truth about the Holy Spirit?

v. 27 Am I willing to use this study as a means to grow in my understanding of the Holy Spirit?

v. 27 What difference has it made in my life to understand that the Holy Spirit is Jesus in me?

v. 27 What has made me feel hopeless about myself? Why do I lack confidence that increasingly others will see Jesus in me? Is it because I am relying on myself for the transformation instead of the Holy Spirit?

STEP 5: Live in Obedient Response to God's Word   *Date:* _____
(What will you do about what God has said?)

I choose to use this study as a means to grow in my understanding of the Holy Spirit, who is Jesus in me; to share this mystery with others; and to live with confident dependence upon the Holy Spirit to change me from glory to glory until others see Jesus in me.

STEP 1
Read God's Word
(Look at the Passage.)

John 14:15–20

15 "If you love me, you will obey what I command.

16 And I will ask the Father, and he will give you another Counselor to be with you forever—

17 the Spirit of truth. The world cannot accept him, because it neither sees him nor knows him. But you know him, for he lives with you and will be in you.

18 I will not leave you as orphans; I will come to you.

19 Before long, the world will not see me anymore, but you will see me. Because I live, you also will live.

20 On that day you will realize that I am in my Father, and you are in me, and I am in you."

STEP 2
What Does God's Word Say?
(List the Facts.)

- **Reread God's Word**
- **List the outstanding facts with verse numbers**
- **Do not paraphrase**

v. 15

v. 16

v. 17

v. 18

v. 19

v. 20

STEP 3
What Does God's Word Mean?
(Learn the Lessons.)

- Write one spiritual lesson for each fact in Step 2.
- Is there an example to follow, a lesson to learn, a command to obey, a warning to heed, a promise to claim?

v. 15

v. 16

v. 17

v. 18

v. 19

v. 20

STEP 4
What Does God's Word Mean in My Life?
(Listen to His Voice.)

- Put the lessons from Step 3 in the form of a question to ask yourself or someone else.

v. 15

v. 16

v. 17

v. 18

v. 19

v. 20

STEP 5: Live in Obedient Response to God's Word   *Date:* _____
(What will you do about what God has said?)

LOVING THE *Person* OF THE HOLY SPIRIT

*One of my deepest, richest joys has been discovering by experience
who the Holy Spirit is in every step of my life's journey.*

—Anne Graham Lotz, *Jesus in Me*, page 9

WEEKLY SCHEDULE

DAY 1   3-Question Study—John 14:21–24

DAY 2   3-Question Study—John 14:25–27

DAY 3   3-Question Study—John 16:5–7

DAY 4   3-Question Study—Romans 8:9–11

DAY 5   3-Question Study—Romans 8:12–17

DAY 6   Reflection, Video Teaching, Group Discussion

Loving the *Person*
of the Holy Spirit

Though you have not seen him, you love him.

—1 Peter 1:8

INDIVIDUAL STUDY INTRODUCTION

I'VE HEARD THE HOLY SPIRIT SPOKEN OF as an "it," a feeling, a dove, a flame of fire, a ghost, an emotion, or even an ecstatic experience. He is referred to as the third Person of the Trinity, as though He is the least of the Trinity, or a postscript to the more significant Father and Son. All of which is inaccurate.

While the Holy Spirit may be symbolized by a dove or flame of fire, while His presence may be accompanied by an emotion or feeling or ecstatic experience, He Himself is distinctly separate from those things. The Holy Spirit is not a thing but a Person.

So at the outset of our exploration of who the Holy Spirit is, keep in mind that He is a living Person who has a mind, a will, and emotions. He is referred to as the third Person of the Trinity not because He is the least, but because He is the third Person to be more fully revealed in Scripture. I can't wait for you to get to know Him better . . .

STEP 1	STEP 2
Read God's Word	What Does God's Word Say?
(Look at the Passage.)	*(List the Facts.)*

John 14:21–24

21 Whoever has my commands and keeps them is the one who loves me. The one who loves me will be loved by my Father, and I too will love them and show myself to them.

22 Then Judas (not Judas Iscariot) said, "But, Lord, why do you intend to show yourself to us and not to the world?"

23 Jesus replied, "Anyone who loves me will obey my teaching. My Father will love them, and we will come to them and make our home with them.

24 Anyone who does not love me will not obey my teaching. These words you hear are not my own; they belong to the Father who sent me.

STEP 3
What Does God's
Word Mean?
(Learn the Lessons.)

STEP 4
What Does God's Word
Mean in My Life?
(Listen to His Voice.)

STEP 5: Live in Obedient Response to God's Word   *Date:* _____
(What will you do about what God has said?)

STEP 1
Read God's Word
(Look at the Passage.)

STEP 2
What Does God's Word Say?
(List the Facts.)

John 14:25–27

25 All this I have spoken while still with you.

26 But the Advocate, the Holy Spirit, whom the
Father will send in my name, will teach you all
things and will remind you of everything I have
said to you.

27 Peace I leave with you; my peace I give you.
I do not give to you as the world gives. Do not
let your hearts be troubled and do not be afraid.

STEP 3
What Does God's Word Mean?
(Learn the Lessons.)

STEP 4
What Does God's Word Mean in My Life?
(Listen to His Voice.)

STEP 5: Live in Obedient Response to God's Word   *Date:* _____

(What will you do about what God has said?)

STEP 1
Read God's Word
(Look at the Passage.)

STEP 2
What Does God's Word Say?
(List the Facts.)

John 16:5–7

5 But now I am going to him who sent me. None of you asks me, 'Where are you going?'

6 Rather, you are filled with grief because I have said these things.

7 But very truly I tell you, it is for your good that I am going away. Unless I go away, the Advocate will not come to you; but if I go, I will send him to you.

STEP 3
What Does God's
Word Mean?
(Learn the Lessons.)

STEP 4
What Does God's Word
Mean in My Life?
(Listen to His Voice.)

STEP 5: Live in Obedient Response to God's Word   *Date:* _____
(What will you do about what God has said?)

STEP 1
Read God's Word
(Look at the Passage.)

STEP 2
What Does God's Word Say?
(List the Facts.)

Romans 8:9–11

9 You, however, are not in the realm of the flesh, but are in the realm of the Spirit, if indeed the Spirit of God lives in you. And if anyone does not have the Spirit of Christ, they do not belong to Christ.

10 But if Christ is in you, then even though your body is subject to death because of sin, the Spirit gives life because of righteousness.

11 And if the Spirit of him who raised Jesus from the dead is living in you, he who raised Christ from the dead will also give life to your mortal bodies because of his Spirit who lives in you.

STEP 3
What Does God's
Word Mean?
(Learn the Lessons.)

STEP 4
What Does God's Word
Mean in My Life?
(Listen to His Voice.)

STEP 5: Live in Obedient Response to God's Word   *Date:* _____
(What will you do about what God has said?)

STEP 1
Read God's Word
(Look at the Passage.)

STEP 2
What Does God's Word Say?
(List the Facts.)

Romans 8:12–17

12 Therefore, brothers and sisters, we have an obligation—but it is not to the flesh, to live according to it.

13 For if you live according to the flesh you will die; but if by the Spirit you put to death the misdeeds of the body, you will live.

14 For those who are led by the Spirit of God are the children of God.

15 The Spirit you received does not make you slaves, so that you live in fear again; rather, the Spirit you received brought about your adoption to sonship. And by him we cry, "*Abba*, Father."

16 The Spirit himself testifies with our spirit, that we are God's children.

17 Now if we are children, then we are heirs— heirs of God and co-heirs with Christ, if indeed we share in his sufferings in order that we may also share in his glory.

STEP 3
What Does God's Word Mean?
(Learn the Lessons.)

STEP 4
What Does God's Word Mean in My Life?
(Listen to His Voice.)

STEP 5: Live in Obedient Response to God's Word
(What will you do about what God has said?)

Date: _____

REFLECTION

Record and journal the following from your study this week about the *Person* of the Holy Spirit.

The Scripture that stood out to you:

The lesson that stood out to you:

The one Live in Obedient Response to God's Word that you committed to this week:

One thing I know for certain:

The Holy Spirit is not an

optional *extra* in my Christian life.

He is a *divine necessity.*

—Anne Graham Lotz,
Jesus in Me, page 3

GROUP STUDY

Welcome to session 2 of the *Jesus in Me* study!

NOTE: You just completed your first week of individual Bible study. If the 3-question study technique was new to your group, consider taking a few moments sharing thoughts on the experience before you dive into this week's video teaching. If anyone has questions or concerns about the individual study time, it is likely someone else feels the same way. Spend the time now to find resolution and answers together, so the remainder of this study can be productive and fruitful for everyone.

My prayer for you as we go through this study is that God Himself will draw near to you and you will experience the constant companionship of the Holy Spirit in a fresh new way. And as a result, you will come to love Him even more.

As we begin, let's open our Bibles and listen for the gentle whispers of the Holy Spirit. The Holy Spirit is wonderful. He is our Helper. He is our Comforter. He is our Counselor. He is our Strengthener. Our Standby. Our Advocate. Our Intercessor. He is another Jesus . . . Jesus living in us.

This week we begin our study by exploring the PERSON of the Holy Spirit.

WATCH VIDEO SESSION 2 (18 MINUTES)

SCRIPTURE IN THIS SESSION:
John 14:2–3, 5–6, 16, John 15:5, 18,
John 16:5–8, 12–16, Numbers 6:24–26, 2 Corinthians 1:4

Use this space to take notes if you like:

GROUP DISCUSSION QUESTIONS

1.   What is something in the video teaching that either was striking or new to you?

2.   Refer to your individual Bible studies this past week. What was one of the most significant lessons you recorded related to the Holy Spirit as a Person and why was it significant? To which verse did it relate?

3.   How does the truth that the Holy Spirit is a Person change your perception of Him? Why do you think it is important to know the Holy Spirit as a living, thinking, feeling Person?

4.   We heard multiple names by which the Holy Spirit is referred to in Scripture. Which of His names is most meaningful to you and why?

WRAP UP

CLOSING PRAYER: Facilitator, pray over your group.

MOVING FORWARD: Review the next week's schedule on the page 32.

BLESSING & ENCOURAGEMENT: Finally, close your group meeting by reading the following blessing and encouragement over them before dismissing.

> *May your heart and mind be softened to the*
> *Person of the Holy Spirit so that he can*
> *"Teach you and remind you of everything Jesus said."*
> —JOHN 14:26

GOING DEEPER

To continue your study of the PERSON OF THE HOLY SPIRIT, read *Jesus in Me: Experiencing the Holy Spirit as a Constant Companion,* Part 1 (pages 5–44).

Enjoying the *Presence* Of the Holy Spirit

As an eternal Person, the Spirit of God has always been present for all time and in all places. In fact, there is no place in the entire universe where He has not, is not, or will not always be fully present. (Psalm 139:7)

—Anne Graham Lotz, *Jesus in Me*, page 53

WEEKLY SCHEDULE

DAY 1   3-Question Study—Genesis 1:1–3

DAY 2   3-Question Study—Acts 1:4–8

DAY 3   3-Question Study—Acts 2:1–8

DAY 4   3-Question Study—Acts 2:14–18

DAY 5   3-Question Study—Acts 2:36–39

DAY 6   Reflection, Video Teaching, Group Discussion

Enjoying the *Presence* of the Holy Spirit

You will fill me with joy in your presence.

—PSALM 16:11

INDIVIDUAL STUDY INTRODUCTION

How many things have been around us for a long time that we simply have not noticed? Like the bagel lever on my toaster. I recently went online to find another toaster because the one I've had for about twenty years no longer toasted both sides of the bread I put into it. When reading the reviews of the brand I was interested in, I came across one purchaser who was pleased that the model she selected toasted one side of her bagel while leaving the other side warm and chewy. I jumped up to see if that could be why my toaster was only toasting half of my bread slices. Sure enough. My toaster had a bagel feature that was turned on. When I turned it off and put in a slice of bread, both sides toasted evenly. I had to laugh, even as I felt foolish for not having noticed the bagel feature that had been there as long as I had owned the toaster.

While toasters are nowhere near the significance of the Holy Spirit, could it be for many of us that we also have never really noticed Him either? Maybe we've never been taught to notice Him. This week we are going to focus in on His presence. Right here. Right now.

STEP 1
Read God's Word
(Look at the Passage.)

STEP 2
What Does God's Word Say?
(List the Facts.)

Genesis 1:1–3

1 In the beginning God created the heavens and the earth.

2 Now the earth was formless and empty, darkness was over the surface of the deep, and the Spirit of God was hovering over the waters.

3 And God said, "Let there be light," and there was light.

STEP 3
What Does God's Word Mean?
(Learn the Lessons.)

STEP 4
What Does God's Word Mean in My Life?
(Listen to His Voice.)

STEP 5: Live in Obedient Response to God's Word   *Date:* _____
(What will you do about what God has said?)

STEP 1
Read God's Word
(Look at the Passage.)

STEP 2
What Does God's Word Say?
(List the Facts.)

Acts 1:4–8

4 On one occasion, while he [Jesus] was eating with them, he gave them this command: "Do not leave Jerusalem, but wait for the gift my Father promised, which you have heard me speak about.

5 For John baptized with water, but in a few days you will be baptized with the Holy Spirit."

6 Then they gathered around him and asked him, "Lord, are you at this time going to restore the kingdom to Israel?"

7 He said to them: "It is not for you to know the times or dates the Father has set by his own authority.

8 But you will receive power when the Holy Spirit comes on you; and you will be my witnesses in Jerusalem, and in all Judea and Samaria, and to the ends of the earth."

STEP 3
What Does God's Word Mean?
(Learn the Lessons.)

STEP 4
What Does God's Word Mean in My Life?
(Listen to His Voice.)

STEP 5: Live in Obedient Response to God's Word   *Date:* _____
(What will you do about what God has said?)

STEP 1
Read God's Word
(Look at the Passage.)

STEP 2
What Does God's Word Say?
(List the Facts.)

Acts 2:1–8

1 When the day of Pentecost came, they were all together in one place.

2 Suddenly a sound like the blowing of a violent wind came from heaven and filled the whole house where they were sitting.

3 They saw what seemed to be tongues of fire that separated and came to rest on each of them.

4 All of them were filled with the Holy Spirit and began to speak in other tongues as the Spirit enabled them.

5 Now there were staying in Jerusalem God-fearing Jews from every nation under heaven.

6 When they heard this sound, a crowd came together in bewilderment, because each one heard their own language being spoken.

7 Utterly amazed, they asked: "Aren't all these who are speaking Galileans?

8 Then how is it that each of us hears them in our native language?"

STEP 3
What Does God's Word Mean?
(Learn the Lessons.)

STEP 4
What Does God's Word Mean in My Life?
(Listen to His Voice.)

STEP 5: Live in Obedient Response to God's Word   Date: _____
(What will you do about what God has said?)

STEP 1
Read God's Word
(Look at the Passage.)

STEP 2
What Does God's Word Say?
(List the Facts.)

Acts 2:14–18

14 Then Peter stood up with the Eleven, raised his voice and addressed the crowd: "Fellow Jews and all of you who live in Jerusalem, let me explain this to you; listen carefully to what I say.

15 These people are not drunk, as you suppose. It's only nine in the morning!

16 No, this is what was spoken by the prophet Joel:

17 In the last days, God says, "I will pour out my Spirit on all people. Your sons and daughters will prophesy, your young men will see visions, your old men will dream dreams.

18 Even on my servants, both men and women, I will pour out my Spirit in those days, and they will prophesy."

STEP 3
What Does God's Word Mean?
(Learn the Lessons.)

STEP 4
What Does God's Word Mean in My Life?
(Listen to His Voice.)

STEP 5: Live in Obedient Response to God's Word   Date: _____
(What will you do about what God has said?)

STEP 1
Read God's Word
(Look at the Passage.)

STEP 2
What Does God's Word Say?
(List the Facts.)

Acts 2:36–39

36 "Therefore let all Israel be assured of this;
God has made this Jesus, whom you
crucified, both Lord and Messiah."

37 When the people heard this, they were cut to
the heart and said to Peter and the other
apostles, "Brothers, what shall we do?"

38 Peter replied, "Repent and be baptized, every
one of you, in the name of Jesus Christ for the
forgiveness of your sins. And you will receive the
gift of the Holy Spirit.

39 The promise is for you and your children and
for all who are far off—for all whom the Lord
our God will call."

STEP 3
What Does God's
Word Mean?
(Learn the Lessons.)

STEP 4
What Does God's Word
Mean in My Life?
(Listen to His Voice.)

STEP 5: Live in Obedient Response to God's Word   *Date:* _____
(What will you do about what God has said?)

REFLECTION

Record and journal the following from your study this week about the PRESENCE of the Holy Spirit.

The Scripture that stood out to you:

The lesson that stood out to you:

The one Live in Obedient Response to God's Word that you committed to this week:

Do you long for faith that really works? Then fully
embrace the Holy Spirit with absolute, total,
unreserved trust, and begin experiencing
His constant presence . . . on the inside.

—Anne Graham Lotz,
Jesus in Me, page 76

GROUP STUDY

Welcome to session 3 of the *Jesus in Me* Bible study!

We continue our study this week exploring the PRESENCE of the Holy Spirit.

Some of us may have made some profound discoveries this week in our individual Bible study time. Some of us may have come to an awareness of the presence of the Holy Spirit we did not previously have. Each of us is on a beautiful journey with the Lord in this study. It is a blessing to share this experience together openly and honestly. Hearing from each other can open our own ears to what the Spirit may be further saying to us!

WATCH VIDEO SESSION 3 (17:30 MINUTES)

SCRIPTURE IN THIS SESSION:
Genesis 1:1–3, John 16:7, Acts 2:6, 1 Samuel 9, Psalm 51:11, Hebrews 13:5, John 14:17

Use this space to take notes if you like:

If you've just prayed with Anne, we'd love to hear from you! Drop us a note at angelmin.info@angelministries.org.

GROUP DISCUSSION QUESTIONS

1. Open your group discussion by sharing something in the video teaching that either was striking or new to you.

2. Refer to your individual Bible studies this past week. What was one of the most significant lessons you recorded related to the presence of the Holy Spirit and why was it significant? To which verse did it relate?

3. What difference did the Holy Spirit make at Creation? Do you think His power is less today?

4. What is most significant to you about the difference between the Old Testament experience of the Holy Spirit and the New Testament experience after Jesus sent Him?

WRAP UP

CLOSING PRAYER: Facilitator, pray over your group.

MOVING FORWARD: Review the next week's schedule on page 52.

BLESSING & ENCOURAGEMENT: Finally, close your group meeting by reading the following blessing and encouragement over them before dismissing.

May you experience a fresh filling of the Holy Spirit this week.
May you be full of worship and
enjoyment and adoration for the One
who was present in the beginning
and has come to live and dwell in you.

GOING DEEPER

To continue your study of THE PRESENCE OF THE HOLY SPIRIT, read *Jesus in Me: Experiencing the Holy Spirit as a Constant Companion*, Part 2 (pages 45–76).

RELYING ON THE *Power* OF THE HOLY SPIRIT

While you have the power of the Holy Spirit within you,
the cooperation of your full surrender, obedience, and faith is required to activate it.

—Anne Graham Lotz, *Jesus in Me*, page 91

WEEKLY SCHEDULE

DAY 1   3-Question Study—Acts 3:1–7

DAY 2   3-Question Study—Acts 4:1–4

DAY 3   3-Question Study—Acts 4:5–13

DAY 4   3-Question Study—Ephesians 3:16–19

DAY 5   3-Question Study—Ephesians 1:15–21

DAY 6   Reflection, Video Teaching, Group Discussion

Relying on the *Power* of the Holy Spirit

"But you will receive power when the Holy Spirit comes on you; and you will be my witness in Jerusalem, and in all Judea and Samaria, and to the ends of the earth."

—Acts 1:8

INDIVIDUAL STUDY INTRODUCTION

ALTHOUGH YOU HAVE ENTERED INTO A PERSONAL RELATIONSHIP with God through faith in Jesus, do you find yourself from time to time running on empty? Are you trying harder to be a "good Christian," putting more and more effort into pleasing God, only to find the desired result elusive? Do you find yourself just going through the motions? Are you attending church and even this Bible study, but increasingly you're living behind a facade, pretending to be more spiritual than you really are? With a fake smile on your lips and the "proper" words on your tongue, are you just trying to make it one more week . . . one more day . . . one more hour . . . one more step? Hoping against hope no one notices, because surely no one else is experiencing this struggle. Is your mind gripped by the thought, "I can't do this? I'm just not cut out to live the Christian life."

Don't be discouraged. There is hope! The One who is within you will enable you to live out the commitment you have made. The key is learning to rely on His power, which is the subject of our study this week.

STEP 1
Read God's Word
(Look at the Passage.)

STEP 2
What Does God's Word Say?
(List the Facts.)

Acts 3:1–7

1 One day Peter and John were going up to the temple at the time of prayer—at three in the afternoon.

2 Now a man who was lame from birth was being carried to the temple gate called Beautiful, where he was put every day to beg from those going into the temple courts.

3 When he saw Peter and John about to enter, he asked them for money.

4 Peter looked straight at him, as did john. Then Peter said, "Look at us!"

5 So the man gave them his attention, expecting to get something from them.

6 Then Peter said, "Silver or gold I do not have, but what I do have I give you. In the name of Jesus Christ of Nazareth walk."

7 Taking him by the right hand, he helped him up, and instantly the man's feet and ankles became strong.

STEP 3
What Does God's
Word Mean?
(Learn the Lessons.)

STEP 4
What Does God's Word
Mean in My Life?
(Listen to His Voice.)

STEP 5: Live in Obedient Response to God's Word   *Date:* _____
(What will you do about what God has said?)

STEP 1
Read God's Word
(Look at the Passage.)

STEP 2
What Does God's Word Say?
(List the Facts.)

Acts 4:1–4

1 The priests and the captain of the temple guard and the Sadducees came up to Peter and John while they were speaking to the people.

2 They were greatly disturbed because the apostles were teaching the people, proclaiming in Jesus the resurrection of the dead.

3 They seized Peter and John and, because it was evening, they put them in jail until the next day.

4 But many who heard the message believed; so the number of men who believed grew to about five thousand.

STEP 3
What Does God's Word Mean?
(Learn the Lessons.)

STEP 4
What Does God's Word Mean in My Life?
(Listen to His Voice.)

STEP 5: Live in Obedient Response to God's Word   Date: _____
(What will you do about what God has said?)

STEP 1
Read God's Word
(Look at the Passage.)

STEP 2
What Does God's Word Say?
(List the Facts.)

Acts 4:5–13

5 The next day the rulers, the elders and the teachers of the law met in Jerusalem.

6 Annas the high priest was there, and so were Caiaphas, John, Alexander and others of the high priest's family.

7 They had Peter and John brought before them and began to question them: "By what power or what name did you do this?"

8 Then Peter, filled with the Holy Spirit, said to them: "Rulers and elders of the people!

9 If we are being called to account today for an act of kindness shown to a man who was lame and are being asked how he was healed,

10 then know this, you and all the people of Israel: It is by the name of Jesus Christ of Nazareth, whom you crucified but whom God raised from the dead, that this man stands before you healed.

11 Jesus is "'the stone you builders rejected, which has become the cornerstone.'

12 Salvation is found in no one else, for there is no other name under heaven given to mankind by which we must be saved."

13 When they saw the courage of Peter and John and realized that they were unschooled, ordinary men, they were astonished and they took note that these men had been with Jesus.

STEP 3
What Does God's
Word Mean?
(Learn the Lessons.)

STEP 4
What Does God's Word
Mean in My Life?
(Listen to His Voice.)

STEP 5: Live in Obedient Response to God's Word   *Date:* _____
(What will you do about what God has said?)

STEP 1
Read God's Word
(Look at the Passage.)

STEP 2
What Does God's Word Say?
(List the Facts.)

Ephesians 3:16–19

16 I pray that out of his glorious riches
   he may strengthen you with power
   through his Spirit in your inner being,

17 So that Christ may dwell in your hearts
   through faith. And I pray that you, being
   rooted and established in love,

18 may have power, together with all the Lord's
   holy people, to grasp how wide and long and
   high and deep is the love of Christ,

19 and to know this love that surpasses knowledge—
   that you may be filled to the measure of all the
   fullness of God.

STEP 3
What Does God's
Word Mean?
(Learn the Lessons.)

STEP 4
What Does God's Word
Mean in My Life?
(Listen to His Voice.)

STEP 5: Live in Obedient Response to God's Word   *Date:* _____
(What will you do about what God has said?)

STEP 1
Read God's Word
(Look at the Passage.)

STEP 2
What Does God's Word Say?
(List the Facts.)

Ephesians 1:15–21

15 For this reason, ever since I heard about
your faith in the Lord Jesus and your love
for all God's people,

16 I have not stopped giving thanks for you,
remembering you in my prayers.

17 I keep asking that the God of our Lord Jesus
Christ, the glorious Father, may give you the
Spirit of wisdom and revelation, so that you may
know him better.

18 I pray that the eyes of your heart may be
enlightened in order that you may know the hope
to which he has called you, the riches of his glorious
inheritance in his holy people,

19 and his incomparably great power for us who believe.
That power is the same as the mighty strength

20 which he exerted in Christ when he raised him from
the dead and seated him at his right hand in the
heavenly realms

21 far above all rule and authority, power and dominion,
and every name that is invoked, not only in the present
age but also in the one to come.

STEP 3
What Does God's Word Mean?
(Learn the Lessons.)

STEP 4
What Does God's Word Mean in My Life?
(Listen to His Voice.)

STEP 5: Live in Obedient Response to God's Word   *Date:* _____
(What will you do about what God has said?)

REFLECTION

Record and journal the following from your study this week about the POWER of the Holy Spirit.

The Scripture that stood out to you:

The lesson that stood out to you:

The one Live in Obedient Response to God's Word that you committed to this week:

When you restrict His access in your life,

you give up being filled with the Spirit

and you deny yourself access to

all His spiritual blessings,

including His power and

eternal purpose for your life.

—Anne Graham Lotz, *Jesus in Me*, page 251

GROUP STUDY

Welcome to session 4 of the *Jesus in Me* Bible study!

This week we have been learning about relying on the POWER of the Holy Spirit and what that power is meant for and how we can better understand it. In today's teaching, Anne will dig into what is required of us practically in order to receive and experience and even wield the power of the Holy Spirit. As we get deeper into this study and explore topics that may still be new to some, may be uncomfortable for others, or may be exhilarating and exciting for yet others, let's commit ourselves to building one another up as Scripture encourages us to do (1 Thessalonians 5:11; Hebrews 3:13; Jude 1:20).

WATCH VIDEO SESSION 4 (17 MINUTES)

SCRIPTURE IN THIS SESSION:
Genesis 1, Ephesians 5:18, 2 Corinthians 3:18,
Acts 2:14–40, Acts 2:37–38, John 16:8–11

SESSION 4

Use this space to take notes if you like:

GROUP DISCUSSION QUESTIONS

1. Open your group discussion by sharing something in the video teaching that either was striking or new to you.

2. Refer to your individual Bible studies this past week. What was one of the most significant lessons you recorded related to the power or transformation given by the Holy Spirit, and why was it significant? To which verse did it relate?

3. Discuss how the Holy Spirit can change someone. How does this impact the way you pray for others? How does this encourage you when you share the gospel?

4. What evidence of the Holy Spirit's filling should others be able to see in your life? Discuss how you can develop in these ways. What would help you to better reflect Jesus?

WRAP UP

CLOSING PRAYER: Facilitator, pray over your group.

MOVING FORWARD: Review the next week's schedule on page 72.

BLESSING & ENCOURAGEMENT: Finally, close your group meeting by reading the following blessing and encouragement over them before dismissing.

> *He gives strength to the weary*
> *and increases the power of the weak.*
> *Even youths grow tired and weary,*
> *and young men stumble and fall;*
> *But those who hope in the LORD*
> *will renew their strength.*
> —ISAIAH 40:29–31 (NIV)

GOING DEEPER

To continue your study of THE POWER OF THE HOLY SPIRIT, read *Jesus in Me: Experiencing the Holy Spirit as a Constant Companion*, Part 3 (pages 77–110).

EMBRACING THE *Purpose* OF THE HOLY SPIRIT

In some ways, our lives are like a symphony. And the Holy Spirit is the conductor. He is the one who brings forth the beautiful music of a life that glorifies God.

—Anne Graham Lotz, *Jesus in Me*, page 115

WEEKLY SCHEDULE

DAY 1   3-Question Study—Matthew 26:31–35

DAY 2   3-Question Study—Matthew 26:69–75

DAY 3   3-Question Study—John 21:15–17

DAY 4   3-Question Study—Ephesians 2:1–5

DAY 5   3-Question Study—Hebrews 10:19–25

DAY 6   Reflection, Video Teaching, Group Discussion

Embracing the *Purpose* of the Holy Spirit

And we all, who with unveiled faces contemplate the Lord's glory,
are being transformed into his image with ever-increasing glory,
which comes from the Lord, who is the Spirit.
—2 Corinthians 3:18

INDIVIDUAL STUDY INTRODUCTION

LIKE ME, HAVE YOU SOMETIMES THOUGHT OF PRIORITIES in the same way you think of New Year's resolutions? A list might look something like this:

- Lose weight
- Start exercising
- Join a gym
- Get in shape
- Drink less Diet Coke
- Drink more water
- Eat less sugar
- Read a book
- Got to bed/get up earlier

Like using a shotgun to shoot a fly, hoping that at least one of the hundreds of bits of buckshot will hit it, we make resolutions hoping to keep at least one of them so we will be better off at the end of the year. The reality is that we rarely keep any of them for the next month, much less the next twelve months.

Sadly, many of us conduct our lives according to this same philosophy. We react to life's challenges and opportunities with no clearly defined purpose, which means we don't have clarity as to how to prioritize our days. In the end, we find ourselves with a life that is at best scattered like buckshot with few worthwhile things to show for it, or is at worst wasted and devoid of eternal significance.

Which is why we need to embrace the Purpose of the Holy Spirit.

STEP 1
Read God's Word
(Look at the Passage.)

STEP 2
What Does God's Word Say?
(List the Facts.)

Matthew 26:31–35

31 Then Jesus told them, "This very night you will all fall away on account of me, for it is written: 'I will strike the shepherd, and the sheep of the flock will be scattered.'

32 But after I have risen, I will go ahead of you into Galilee."

33 Peter replied, "Even if all fall away on account of you, I never will."

34 "Truly I tell you," Jesus answered, "this very night, before the rooster crows, you will disown me three times."

35 But Peter declared, "Even if I have to die with you, I will never disown you." And all the other disciples said the same.

STEP 3
What Does God's Word Mean?
(Learn the Lessons.)

STEP 4
What Does God's Word Mean in My Life?
(Listen to His Voice.)

STEP 5: Live in Obedient Response to God's Word   *Date:* _____
(What will you do about what God has said?)

STEP 1
Read God's Word
(Look at the Passage.)

STEP 2
What Does God's Word Say?
(List the Facts.)

Matthew 26:69–75

69 Now Peter was sitting out in the courtyard, and a servant girl came to him. "You also were with Jesus of Galilee," she said.

70 But he denied it before them all. "I don't know what you're talking about," he said.

71 Then he went out to the gateway, where another servant girl saw him and said to the people there, "This fellow was with Jesus of Nazareth."

72 He denied it again, with an oath: "I don't know the man!"

73 After a little while, those standing there went up to Peter and said, "Surely you are one of them; your accent gives you away."

74 Then he began to call down curses, and he swore to them, "I don't know the man!" Immediately a rooster crowed.

75 Then Peter remembered the word Jesus had spoken: "Before the rooster crows, you will disown me three times." And he went outside and wept bitterly.

STEP 3
What Does God's
Word Mean?
(Learn the Lessons.)

STEP 4
What Does God's Word
Mean in My Life?
(Listen to His Voice.)

STEP 5: Live in Obedient Response to God's Word   *Date:* _____
(What will you do about what God has said?)

STEP 1
Read God's Word
(Look at the Passage.)

STEP 2
What Does God's Word Say?
(List the Facts.)

John 21:15–17

15 When they had finished eating, Jesus said to
Simon Peter, "Simon son of John, do you love
me more than these?" "Yes, Lord," he said,
"you know that I love you." Jesus said,
"Feed my lambs."

16 Again Jesus said, "Simon son of John, do you
love me?" He answered, "Yes, Lord, you know
that I love you." Jesus said, "Take care of my sheep."

17 The third time he said to him, "Simon son of John,
do you love me?" Peter was hurt because Jesus
asked him the third time, "Do you love me?"
He said, "Lord, you know all things; you know
that I love you." Jesus said, "Feed my sheep."

STEP 3
What Does God's Word Mean?
(Learn the Lessons.)

STEP 4
What Does God's Word Mean in My Life?
(Listen to His Voice.)

STEP 5: Live in Obedient Response to God's Word   *Date:* _____
(What will you do about what God has said?)

STEP 1
Read God's Word
(Look at the Passage.)

STEP 2
What Does God's Word Say?
(List the Facts.)

Ephesians 2:1–5

1 As for you, you were dead in your
   transgressions and sins,

2 In which you used to live when you followed
   the ways of this world and of the ruler of the
   kingdom of the air, the spirit who is now at
   work in those who are disobedient.

3 All of us also lived among them at one time,
   gratifying the cravings of our flesh and
   following its desires and thoughts. Like the rest,
   we were by nature deserving of wrath.

4 But because of his great love for us, God,
   who is rich in mercy,

5 made us alive with Christ even when we
   were dead in transgressions—it is by grace
   you have been saved.

STEP 3
What Does God's Word Mean?
(Learn the Lessons.)

STEP 4
What Does God's Word Mean in My Life?
(Listen to His Voice.)

STEP 5: Live in Obedient Response to God's Word   *Date:* _____
(What will you do about what God has said?)

STEP 1
Read God's Word
(Look at the Passage.)

STEP 2
What Does God's Word Say?
(List the Facts.)

Hebrews 10:19–25

19 Therefore, brothers and sisters, since we have confidence to enter the Most Holy Place by the blood of Jesus,

20 by a new and living way opened for us through the curtain, that is, his body,

21 and since we have a great priest over the house of God,

22 let us draw near to God with a sincere heart and with the full assurance that faith brings, having our hearts sprinkled to cleanse us from a guilty conscience and having our bodies washed with pure water.

23 Let us hold unswervingly to the hope we profess, for he who promised is faithful.

24 And let us consider how we may spur one another on toward love and good deeds,

25 not giving up meeting together, as some are in the habit of doing, but encouraging one another—and all the more as you see the Day approaching.

STEP 3
What Does God's Word Mean?
(Learn the Lessons.)

STEP 4
What Does God's Word Mean in My Life?
(Listen to His Voice.)

STEP 5: Live in Obedient Response to God's Word   *Date:* _____
(What will you do about what God has said?)

REFLECTION

Record and journal the following from your study this week about the PURPOSE of the Holy Spirit.

The Scripture that stood out to you:

The lesson that stood out to you:

The one Live in Obedient Response to God's Word that you committed to this week:

Jesus promised that "He will guide you into all truth." So, ask Him to guide your focus until it's laser-like in steadfast resolution to bring God glory in all you say and do. Then relax. Regardless of whatever life may bring your way, embrace the Spirit's purpose.

—Anne Graham Lotz, *Jesus in Me*, page 129

GROUP STUDY

Welcome to session 5 of the *Jesus in Me* Bible study!

Does the purpose for which you have been living challenge you? Does it fulfill you? Or have you sensed a restless emptiness deep within? Have you longed to live for something more, bigger, or greater?

Where does that desire for something greater come from? Why are we stirred to yearn for a life that is more than ordinary? One reason is that we are created in the image of God with the capacity to know Him in a personal, permanent relationship for the purpose of bringing Him glory. Until that purpose is fulfilled, we will be empty, deeply dissatisfied and unfulfilled as we continually try to fill the void with substitutes.

But if you have established a personal relationship with God and you still feel unfulfilled and dissatisfied, it could be that the Holy Spirit is stirring you up, trying to direct your attention to your life's purpose.

This week we have transitioned from the "who" to the "for what", as we learn about the PURPOSE of the Holy Spirit.

WATCH VIDEO SESSION 5 (15 MINUTES)

SCRIPTURE IN THIS SESSION:
Genesis 12:1, 2 Chronicles 20:7, Isaiah 41:8,
James 2:23, Ephesians 1:6, 2:10, Genesis 50, Romans 8:28

Use this space to take notes if you like:

GROUP DISCUSSION QUESTIONS

1. Open your group discussion by sharing something in the video teaching that either was striking or new to you.

2. Refer to your individual Bible studies this past week. What was one of the most significant lessons you recorded related to the purpose of the Holy Spirit, and why was it significant? To which verse did it relate?

3. After being together for five sessions, what spiritual gifts do you see in each other? How can you use your spiritual gifts to build each other up?

4. In what ways is your confidence in God strengthened more in times of comfort or in times of crisis? What conflict, chaos, and disruption could be part of God's purpose to strengthen your faith?

WRAP UP

CLOSING PRAYER: Facilitator, pray over your group.

MOVING FORWARD: Review the next week's schedule on page 92.

BLESSING & ENCOURAGEMENT: Finally, close your group meeting by reading the following blessing and encouragement over them before dismissing.

> *May the Holy Spirit guide you in steadfast resolution*
> *to know God and embrace the Spirit's purpose*
> *for you to glorify Him in all you say and in all you do.*

GOING DEEPER

To continue your study of THE PURPOSE OF THE HOLY SPIRIT, read *Jesus in Me: Experiencing the Holy Spirit as a Constant Companion,* Part 4 (pages 111–148).

LIVING BY THE *Precepts* OF THE HOLY SPIRIT

*My love of reading, studying, applying, and obeying my Bible
has led me to the deep conviction that it is more than just great literature.
There is something supernatural about it. It works!*

—Anne Graham Lotz, *Jesus in Me*, page 153

WEEKLY SCHEDULE

Day 1   3-Question Study—Matthew 4:1–4

Day 2   3-Question Study—Matthew 4:5–11

Day 3   3-Question Study—2 Timothy 3:14–17

Day 4   3-Question Study—1 John 2:3–6

Day 5   3-Question Study—Psalm 1

Day 6   Reflection, Video Teaching, Group Discussion

Living by the *Precepts*
of the Holy Spirit

All Scripture is God-breathed and is useful for teaching, rebuking,
correcting and training in righteousness . . .
—2 Timothy 3:16

INDIVIDUAL STUDY INTRODUCTION

WHILE I OWNED SOME CHILD-FRIENDLY VERSIONS of the Bible when growing up, my first "real" Bible was a navy, leather-bound, King James Version, Scofield edition. Mother and Daddy gave it to me at my baptism. It is a treasure that I still have safely on my bookshelf. In the flyleaf, my mother wrote these words:

"To Anne– (who on this January 13, 1957 publicly took her stand for Christ, her Savior), we give this Book, your one sure guide in an unsure world. Read it, study it, love it, live it. In it you will find a verse for every occasion. Hide them in your heart."

Although my mother's words were written over sixty years ago, their wisdom transcends generations, cultures, world events, time, and age.

My love of reading, studying, applying, and obeying my Bible has led me to the deep conviction that it is more than just great literature. There is something supernatural about it. It works! It pulsates with life! How could that be? What makes it so unique? The answer to those questions leads us straight to the Holy Spirit.

STEP 1
Read God's Word
(Look at the Passage.)

STEP 2
What Does God's Word Say?
(List the Facts.)

Matthew 4:1–4

1 Then Jesus was led by the Spirit into the wilderness to be tempted by the devil.

2 After fasting forty days and forty nights, he was hungry.

3 The tempter came to him and said, "If you are the Son of God, tell these stones to become bread."

4 Jesus answered, "It is written: 'Man shall not live on bread alone, but on every word that comes from the mouth of God.'"

STEP 3
What Does God's Word Mean?
(Learn the Lessons.)

STEP 4
What Does God's Word Mean in My Life?
(Listen to His Voice.)

STEP 5: Live in Obedient Response to God's Word   *Date:* _____
(What will you do about what God has said?)

STEP 1
Read God's Word
(Look at the Passage.)

STEP 2
What Does God's Word Say?
(List the Facts.)

Matthew 4:5–11

5 Then the devil took him to the holy city and had him stand on the highest point of the temple.

6 "If you are the Son of God," he said, "throw yourself down. For it is written: 'He will command his angels concerning you, and they will lift you up in their hands, so that you will not strike your foot against a stone.'"

7 Jesus answered him, "It is also written: 'Do not put the Lord your God to the test.'"

8 Again, the devil took him to a very high mountain and showed him all the kingdoms of the world and their splendor.

9 "All this I will give you," he said, "if you will bow down and worship me."

10 Jesus said to him, "Away from me, Satan! For it is written: 'Worship the Lord your God and serve him only.'"

11 Then the devil left him, and angels came and attended him.

STEP 3
What Does God's
Word Mean?
(*Learn the Lessons.*)

STEP 4
What Does God's Word
Mean in My Life?
(*Listen to His Voice.*)

STEP 5: Live in Obedient Response to God's Word   *Date:* _____
(*What will you do about what God has said?*)

STEP 1
Read God's Word
(Look at the Passage.)

2 Timothy 3:14–17

14 But as for you, continue in what you have learned and have become convinced of, because you know those from whom you learned it,

15 and how from infancy you have known the Holy Scriptures, which are able to make you wise for salvation through faith in Christ Jesus.

16 All Scripture is God-breathed, and is useful for teaching, rebuking, correcting and training in righteousness,

17 so that the servant of God may be thoroughly equipped for every good work.

STEP 2
What Does God's Word Say?
(List the Facts.)

STEP 3
What Does God's
Word Mean?
(Learn the Lessons.)

STEP 4
What Does God's Word
Mean in My Life?
(Listen to His Voice.)

STEP 5: Live in Obedient Response to God's Word   *Date:* _____

(What will you do about what God has said?)

STEP 1
Read God's Word
(Look at the Passage.)

STEP 2
What Does God's Word Say?
(List the Facts.)

1 John 2:3–6

3 We know that we have come to know him if we keep his commands.

4 Whoever says, "I know him," but does not do what he commands is a liar, and the truth is not in that person.

5 But if anyone obeys his word, love for God is truly made complete in them. This is how we know we are in him.

6 Whoever claims to live in him must live as Jesus did.

STEP 3
What Does God's
Word Mean?
(Learn the Lessons.)

STEP 4
What Does God's Word
Mean in My Life?
(Listen to His Voice.)

STEP 5: Live in Obedient Response to God's Word   *Date:* _____
(What will you do about what God has said?)

STEP 1
Read God's Word
(Look at the Passage.)

STEP 2
What Does God's Word Say?
(List the Facts.)

Psalm 1:1–6

1 Blessed is the one who does not walk in step
with the wicked or stand in the way that
sinners take or sit in the company of mockers,

2 but whose delight is in the law of the LORD, and
who meditates on his law day and night.

3 That person is like a tree planted by streams of
water, which yields its fruit in season and whose
leaf does not wither—whatever they do prospers.

4 Not so the wicked! They are like chaff that
the wind blows away.

5 Therefore the wicked will not stand in the
judgment, nor sinners in the assembly of
the righteous.

6 For the LORD watches over the way of the
righteous, but the way of the wicked leads
to destruction.

STEP 3
What Does God's Word Mean?
(Learn the Lessons.)

STEP 4
What Does God's Word Mean in My Life?
(Listen to His Voice.)

STEP 5: Live in Obedient Response to God's Word   Date: _____
(What will you do about what God has said?)

REFLECTION

Record and journal the following from your study this week about the PRECEPTS of the Holy Spirit.

The Scripture that stood out to you:

The lesson that stood out to you:

The one Live in Obedient Response to God's Word that you committed to this week:

This exercise [of Bible study] is simple
but challenging in that it requires you and me to think
for ourselves. It effectively removes the "middleman"
and allows us to hear directly from the
Spirit through God's Word.

—Anne Graham Lotz, *Jesus in Me*, page 246

GROUP STUDY

Welcome to session 6 of the Jesus in Me Bible study!

All Scripture from Genesis to Revelation is God-breathed because it is inspired by the Holy Spirit—the Spirit of Truth. So regardless of the way you were raised, what is your opinion of the Bible now and how was that opinion formed? Have you been influenced by others who are critical? Have you been taught that it is a good book that contains God's Word, but it is not God's Word in its entirety? Have you been told that the Bible contains errors or myths?

Whatever your opinion about the Bible has been up until this moment, I want to challenge you to decide now, once and for all, that you believe it. Why? *Because it is God's Word. It is backed by His character.*

Read it and live it out for yourself. You will discover the same thing that I discovered. The Bible works. Then choose to place your faith in the Bible as being true, inspired, and infallible. Follow the Creator's directions for life. Live by the precepts of the Holy Spirit.

We praise God that you are persevering and endeavoring to experience the Holy Spirit as a constant companion!

WATCH VIDEO SESSION 6 (16:30 MINUTES)

SCRIPTURE IN THIS SESSION:
John 16:13, 2 Timothy 3:16, Revelation 19,
Jeremiah 36:4, 16–24, 27–39,
Genesis 3:1, Matthew 5:18, 2 Kings 5

Use this space to take notes if you like:

GROUP DISCUSSION QUESTIONS

1. Open your group discussion by sharing something in the video teaching that either was striking or new to you.

2. Refer to your individual Bible studies this past week. What was one of the most significant lessons you recorded on the precepts of the Holy Spirit, and why was it significant? To which verse did it relate?

3. In order to live by God's precepts and follow His directions for living, we must read them. How do you structure your daily time in God's Word? Share any helpful ideas with the group.

4. Make a list of practical steps you will take today to start following God's directions more closely. Consider challenges and obstacles and outright opposition you may encounter. How can you be prepared to follow through?

WRAP UP

CLOSING PRAYER: Facilitator, pray over your group.

MOVING FORWARD: Review the next week's schedule on page 112.

BLESSING & ENCOURAGEMENT: Finally, close your group meeting by reading the following blessing and encouragement over them before dismissing.

May you receive and trust the Word of Jesus:

"But when He, the Spirit of Truth comes,
He will guide you into all truth."

—JOHN 16:13

GOING DEEPER

To continue your study of THE PRECEPTS OF THE HOLY SPIRIT, read *Jesus in Me: Experiencing the Holy Spirit as a Constant Companion,* Part 5 (pages 149–166).

REFLECTING THE *Purity*
OF THE HOLY SPIRIT

*I believe the church today is in desperate need of revival. Authentic revival.
Not a tent meeting or a series of services to save the lost, but a spiritual awakening that will
compel God's people to repent of our sin, return to the cross,
and recommit ourselves to living lives that reflect His purity.*

—Anne Graham Lotz, *Jesus in Me*, page 174

WEEKLY SCHEDULE

DAY 1   3-Question Study—Acts 5:1–6

DAY 2   3-Question Study—Acts 5:7–11

DAY 3   3-Question Study—1 John 1:5–10

DAY 4   3-Question Study—Philippians 1:9–11

DAY 5   3-Question Study—1 Peter 1:13–16

DAY 6 · Reflection, Video Teaching, Group Discussion

Reflecting the *Purity* of the Holy Spirit

Set an example for the believers in speech, in life, in love, in faith and in purity.
—1 Timothy 4:12

INDIVIDUAL STUDY INTRODUCTION

Y OU AND I LIVE SURROUNDED BY A CULTURE that has become spiritually and morally bankrupt. Right has been replaced with wrong, and wrong is now the new right. Infanticide and abortion, assisted suicide, gay marriage, pornography, sexting, gender identity, euthanasia, sex slavery, date rape, road rage, obscenity, obsession with self, greed, cruelty, the glorification of violence through video games and rap music . . . the evidence is overwhelming that there seems to be no regard for holiness or purity.

The distressing thing I've observed is that there seems to be less and less regard for purity within the church! The church, generally speaking, seems to be absorbing the world around us instead of separating from it. The result is that the holiness of God is not always reflected in the way Christians think, live, speak, and act. Yet we are clearly commanded to "be holy as He is holy" (1 Peter 1:15). And we are warned that without holiness, no one will see the Lord. (Hebrews 12:14)

God takes sin seriously. It's time we did too. This week we will focus on the characteristic that is so much a part of the Spirit of God it's reflected in His name . . . the *Holy* Spirit.

STEP 1
Read God's Word
(Look at the Passage.)

STEP 2
What Does God's Word Say?
(List the Facts.)

Acts 5:1–6

1 Now a man named Ananias, together with his wife Sapphira, also sold a piece of property.

2 With his wife's full knowledge he kept back part of the money for himself, but brought the rest and put it at the apostles' feet.

3 Then Peter said, "Ananias, how is it that Satan has so filled your heart that you have lied to the Holy Spirit and have kept for yourself some of the money you received for the land?

4 Didn't it belong to you before it was sold? And after it was sold, wasn't the money at your disposal? What made you think of doing such a thing? You have not lied just to human beings but to God."

5 When Ananias heard this, he fell down and died. And great fear seized all who heard what had happened.

6 Then some young men came forward, wrapped up his body, and carried him out and buried him.

STEP 3
What Does God's Word Mean?
(Learn the Lessons.)

STEP 4
What Does God's Word Mean in My Life?
(Listen to His Voice.)

STEP 5: Live in Obedient Response to God's Word   *Date:* _____
(What will you do about what God has said?)

STEP 1
Read God's Word
(Look at the Passage.)

Acts 5:7–11

7 About three hours later his wife came in, not knowing what had happened.

8 Peter asked her, "Tell me, is this the price you and Ananias got for the land?" "Yes," she said, "that is the price."

9 Peter said to her, "How could you conspire to test the Spirit of the Lord? Listen! The feet of the men who buried your husband are at the door, and they will carry you out also."

10 At that moment she fell down at his feet and died. Then the young men came in and, finding her dead, carried her out and buried her beside her husband.

11 Great fear seized the whole church and all who heard about these events.

STEP 2
What Does God's Word Say?
(List the Facts.)

STEP 3
What Does God's
Word Mean?
(Learn the Lessons.)

STEP 4
What Does God's Word
Mean in My Life?
(Listen to His Voice.)

STEP 5: Live in Obedient Response to God's Word   *Date:* _____
(What will you do about what God has said?)

STEP 1
Read God's Word
(Look at the Passage.)

STEP 2
What Does God's Word Say?
(List the Facts.)

1 John 1:5–10

5 This is the message we have heard from him and declare to you: God is light; in him there is no darkness at all.

6 If we claim to have fellowship with him and yet walk in the darkness, we lie and do not live out the truth.

7 But if we walk in the light, as he is in the light, we have fellowship with one another, and the blood of Jesus, his Son, purifies us from all sin.

8 If we claim to be without sin, we deceive ourselves and the truth is not in us.

9 If we confess our sins, he is faithful and just and will forgive us our sins and purify us from all unrighteousness.

10 If we claim we have not sinned, we make him out to be a liar and his word is not in us.

STEP 3
What Does God's Word Mean?
(Learn the Lessons.)

STEP 4
What Does God's Word Mean in My Life?
(Listen to His Voice.)

STEP 5: Live in Obedient Response to God's Word   *Date:* _____
(What will you do about what God has said?)

STEP 1
Read God's Word
(Look at the Passage.)

STEP 2
What Does God's Word Say?
(List the Facts.)

Philippians 1:9–11

9 And this is my prayer: that your love may abound more and more in knowledge and depth of insight,

10 so that you may be able to discern what is best and may be pure and blameless for the day of Christ,

11 filled with the fruit of righteousness that comes through Jesus Christ—to the glory and praise of God.

STEP 3
What Does God's Word Mean?
(Learn the Lessons.)

STEP 4
What Does God's Word Mean in My Life?
(Listen to His Voice.)

STEP 5: Live in Obedient Response to God's Word   *Date:* _____
(What will you do about what God has said?)

STEP 1
Read God's Word
(Look at the Passage.)

STEP 2
What Does God's Word Say?
(List the Facts.)

1 Peter 1:13–16

13 Therefore, with minds that are alert and fully sober, set your hope on the grace to be brought to you when Jesus Christ is revealed at his coming.

14 As obedient children, do not conform to the evil desires you had when you lived in ignorance.

15 But just as he who called you is holy, so be holy in all you do;

16 for it is written: "Be holy, because I am holy."

STEP 3
What Does God's Word Mean?
(Learn the Lessons.)

STEP 4
What Does God's Word Mean in My Life?
(Listen to His Voice.)

STEP 5: Live in Obedient Response to God's Word   *Date:* _____

(What will you do about what God has said?)

REFLECTION

Record and journal the following from your study this week about the PURITY of the Holy Spirit.

The Scripture that stood out to you:

The lesson that stood out to you:

The one Live in Obedient Response to God's Word that you committed to this week:

What has happened to purity? Within the church?
Within the lives of those who call themselves by God's
name? Is the lack of purity an indication that the Holy
Spirit is withdrawing Himself?

—Anne Graham Lotz, *Jesus In Me*, page 170

GROUP STUDY

Welcome to the seventh week of the *Jesus in Me* study! What a blessing to continue on this journey and to grow in faith alongside each other.

This past week may have been a bit of a challenge for some of us. Often when we consider the difference between the holiness of God and our human, sinful state we are met with some uncomfortable and troubling truths. It takes courage to see ourselves, not as we think we are or as others say we are, but as God sees us.

The purity of the Holy Spirit is our plumb line. God measures us by the holiness of His Spirit, not in comparison with others. And He commands us to be holy as He is holy. The encouraging truth is that the Holy Spirit within us takes on the responsibility of purifying our lives.

Purification is a process, so be patient with one another and in love, encourage, listen, discuss, and share for the benefit of those in your group.

WATCH VIDEO SESSION 7 (21 MINUTES)

SCRIPTURE IN THIS SESSION:
John 14:26, 1 Peter 1:16, Leviticus 11:44–45; 19:2,
John 16:8, 1 John 1:8–9

Use this space to take notes if you like:

GROUP DISCUSSION QUESTIONS

1. Open your group discussion by sharing something in the video teaching that was either striking or was new to you.

2. Refer to your personal Bible studies this past week. What was one of the most significant lessons you recorded on the purity of the Holy Spirit, and why was it significant? To which verse did it relate?

3. From the list of sins, did you spot a "no-see-um" that you would be willing to share? What do you need to put in or put out of your life?

4. Have your beliefs or your understanding of what it is to be holy changed in this session? In what ways? What has most impacted your understanding of holiness?

WRAP UP

CLOSING PRAYER: Facilitator, pray over your group.

MOVING FORWARD: Review the next week's schedule on page 132.

BLESSING & ENCOURAGEMENT: Finally, close your group meeting by reading the following blessing and encouragement over them before dismissing.

May you be blessed by the care and love
of the Holy Spirit whose heart is to
transform you more into His likeness
and share his purity and holiness to the glory of God.

GOING DEEPER

To continue your study of THE PURITY OF THE HOLY SPIRIT, read *Jesus in Me: Experiencing the Holy Spirit as a Constant Companion,* Part 6 (pages 167–194).

TRUSTING IN THE *Priority* OF THE HOLY SPIRIT

. . . remember that the Holy Spirit is praying for you. Specifically. Personally. With full understanding and a heart of love.

Anne Graham Lotz, *Jesus in Me*, page 223

WEEKLY SCHEDULE

DAY 1   3-Question Study—John 4:7–10

DAY 2   3-Question Study—John 4:28–30, 39, 42

DAY 3   3-Question Study—Romans 8:22–28

DAY 4   3-Question Study—1 Corinthians 2:11–16

DAY 5   3-Question Study—2 Corinthians 3:15–18

DAY 6   Reflection, Video Teaching, Group Discussion

Trusting in the *Priority* of the Holy Spirit

"I have much more to say to you, more than you can now bear. But when he, the Spirit of truth, comes, he will guide you into all the truth. He will not speak on his own; he will speak only what he hears, and he will tell you what is yet to come."

—John 16:12–13

INDIVIDUAL STUDY INTRODUCTION

The priority of the Holy Spirit is to guide us into all truth—truth revealed in the written Word of God so that we might know the living Word of God who is Jesus . . . the truth incarnate. The purpose, the goal, and the priority of the Holy Spirit can be summed up in one word: JESUS. When we wrap our minds around the laser-like focus of the Holy Spirit, a lot of things seem to make sense, including the Bible itself. I pray that this study has not only taught you about the Holy Spirit, but opened your eyes to God's Word and your ears to His voice.

As we conclude, remember that the Holy Spirit loves you! He cares deeply about what you care about because He cares about you. It doesn't matter how small or how large your "care" is, He cares. He understands. He wants what's best for you. He desires for you to fulfill your God-given potential. He wants to ease your burden, solve your problem, comfort your broken heart, bind up your wounds, bring you through the valley of the shadow, shower you with blessing upon blessing . . . and yes, He wants to make you holy . . . because He loves you! So relax. Stop trying to impress Him. Stop working so hard to earn His love. Be open and honest and transparent. Live your life with the confidence that you are deeply, unconditionally, permanently loved by Him. You can trust Him. Just trust Him.

STEP 1
Read God's Word
(Look at the Passage.)

STEP 2
What Does God's Word Say?
(List the Facts.)

John 4:7–10

7 When a Samaritan woman came to draw water, Jesus said to her, "Will you give me a drink?"

8 (His disciples had gone into town to buy food.)

9 The Samaritan woman said to him, "You are a Jew and I am a Samaritan woman. How can you ask me for a drink?" (For Jews do not associate with Samaritans.)

10 Jesus answered her, "If you knew the gift of God and who it is that asks you for a drink, you would have asked him and he would have given you living water."

STEP 3
What Does God's
Word Mean?
(Learn the Lessons.)

STEP 4
What Does God's Word
Mean in My Life?
(Listen to His Voice.)

STEP 5: Live in Obedient Response to God's Word   *Date:* _____
(What will you do about what God has said?)

STEP 1
Read God's Word
(Look at the Passage.)

STEP 2
What Does God's Word Say?
(List the Facts.)

John 4:28–30, 39, 42

28 Then, leaving her water jar, the woman went back to the town and said to the people,

29 "Come, see a man who told me everything I ever did. Could this be the Messiah?"

30 They came out of the town and made their way toward him.

39 Many of the Samaritans from that town believed in him because of the woman's testimony, "He told me everything I ever did."

42 They said to the woman, "We no longer believe just because of what you said; now we have heard for ourselves, and we know that this man really is the Savior of the world."

STEP 3
What Does God's Word Mean?
(Learn the Lessons.)

STEP 4
What Does God's Word Mean in My Life?
(Listen to His Voice.)

STEP 5: Live in Obedient Response to God's Word   *Date:* _____
(What will you do about what God has said?)

STEP 1
Read God's Word
(Look at the Passage.)

STEP 2
What Does God's Word Say?
(List the Facts.)

Romans 8:22–28

22 We know that the whole creation has been
groaning as in the pains of childbirth
right up to the present time.

23 Not only so, but we ourselves, who have the
firstfruits of the Spirit, groan inwardly as we
wait eagerly for our adoption to sonship, the
redemption of our bodies.

24 For in this hope we were saved. But hope that
is seen is no hope at all. Who hopes for what
they already have?

25 But if we hope for what we do not yet have,
we wait for it patiently.

26 In the same way, the Spirit helps us in our
weakness. We do not know what we ought
to pray for, but the Spirit himself intercedes
for us through wordless groans.

27 And he who searches our hearts knows the mind
of the Spirit, because the Spirit intercedes for God's
people in accordance with the will of God.

28 And we know that in all things God works for the
good of those who love him, who have been called
according to his purpose.

STEP 3
What Does God's Word Mean?
(Learn the Lessons.)

STEP 4
What Does God's Word Mean in My Life?
(Listen to His Voice.)

STEP 5: Live in Obedient Response to God's Word   *Date:* _____
(What will you do about what God has said?)

STEP 1	STEP 2
Read God's Word	**What Does God's Word Say?**
(Look at the Passage.)	*(List the Facts.)*

1 Corinthians 2:11–16

11 For who knows a person's thoughts except their own spirit within them? In the same way no one knows the thoughts of God except the Spirit of God.

12 What we have received is not the spirit of the world, but the Spirit who is from God, so that we may understand what God has freely given us.

13 This is what we speak, not in words taught us by human wisdom but in words taught by the Spirit, explaining spiritual realities with Spirit-taught words.

14 The person without the Spirit does not accept the things that come from the Spirit of God but considers them foolishness, and cannot understand them because they are discerned only through the Spirit.

15 The person with the Spirit makes judgments about all things, but such a person is not subject to merely human judgments,

16 for, "Who has known the mind of the Lord so as to instruct him?" But we have the mind of Christ.

STEP 3
What Does God's
Word Mean?
(Learn the Lessons.)

STEP 4
What Does God's Word
Mean in My Life?
(Listen to His Voice.)

STEP 5: Live in Obedient Response to God's Word   *Date:* _____
(What will you do about what God has said?)

STEP 1
Read God's Word
(Look at the Passage.)

STEP 2
What Does God's Word Say?
(List the Facts.)

2 Corinthians 3:15–18

15 Even to this day when Moses is read,
a veil covers their hearts.

16 But whenever anyone turns to the
Lord, the veil is taken away.

17 Now the Lord is the Spirit, and where
the Spirit of the Lord is, there is freedom.

18 And we all, who with unveiled faces
contemplate the Lord's glory, are being
transformed into his image, with
ever-increasing glory, which comes
from the Lord, who is the Spirit.

STEP 3
What Does God's Word Mean?
(Learn the Lessons.)

STEP 4
What Does God's Word Mean in My Life?
(Listen to His Voice.)

STEP 5: Live in Obedient Response to God's Word   *Date:* _____
(What will you do about what God has said?)

REFLECTION

Record and journal the following from your study this week about the PRIORITY of the Holy Spirit.

The Scripture that stood out to you:

The lesson that stood out to you:

The one Live in Obedient Response to God's Word that you committed to this week:

Jesus is the reason for everything that exists,

including you and me. He is our ultimate purpose,

our ultimate goal, and our ultimate priority.

If your life's purpose, goal, and priorities

are about anything less than Jesus only,

anything other than Jesus only,

anything more than Jesus only,

then there is a disconnect between you

and the Holy Spirit. Because, remember,

the Holy Spirit's ultimate purpose is to glorify Jesus,

His ultimate goal is to make Jesus known to you

and to me, and His priority is to

guide us into all truth as

He transforms us into the image of Jesus.

—Anne Graham Lotz, *Jesus in Me*, page 238

GROUP STUDY

Welcome to the final week of our Jesus in Me Bible study!

What difference has this study made in your habits? Your daily or weekly schedule? Your thinking? What has made it worth your time and effort?

Share with your group what you have enjoyed most about this group study. As you gather this week, take time to express your gratitude for all the Holy Spirit has taught you, shown you, and revealed to you. Take a moment to reflect on the fact that the Holy Spirit is Jesus. In you! He will be your constant companion as you leave this study, and one day will present you faultless before the Father. To the praise of His glory!

WATCH VIDEO SESSION 8 (21:30 MINUTES)

SCRIPTURE IN THIS SESSION
Romans 8:26, Ephesians 4:30, John 16:13–14,
Genesis 1:2–3, John 1:14, Colossians 1:16, Genesis 2–5, 18, 32,
Joshua 5–6, Daniel 3, Isaiah 43:2, Psalm 23:4,
Isaiah 6, Ezekiel, Luke 2, 24, Revelation 19

Use this space to take notes if you like:

GROUP DISCUSSION QUESTIONS

1. Open your group discussion by sharing something in the video that was either striking or was new to you.

2. Refer to your personal Bible studies this past week. What was one of the most significant lessons you recorded on the priority of the Holy Spirit, and why was it significant? To which verse did it relate? Without the Spirit's clarity, how does the world view Jesus?

3. Turn to John 16:13 in your Bibles. Discuss practical ways we can apply John 16:13 to a person's struggle to understand God's Word.

4. Who is the subject of the Bible according to Luke 24:27? Why is this so relevant to our understanding of the Bible? What are we missing if we overlook this one key fact?

WRAP UP

CLOSING PRAYER: Facilitator, pray over your group.

BLESSING & ENCOURAGEMENT: Then, close your group meeting by reading the following blessing and encouragement over them before dismissing.

*May the Holy Spirit guide you into all truth,
keep you from distraction, doubt, discouragement,
and disobedience. May you continue to know Jesus,
love Jesus, and trust Jesus so that you
can bring glory to Him.*

What are some ways you can tell others who the Holy Spirit is? Consider hosting a Bible study group yourself using this curriculum. Who can you invite? Who do you know that would benefit from this study?

GOING DEEPER

To continue your study of THE PRIORITY OF THE HOLY SPIRIT, read *Jesus in Me: Experiencing the Holy Spirit as a Constant Companion,* Part 7 and Conclusion (pages 195–239).

SESSION 8

CLOSING PRAYER

My prayer for you as you conclude your study of Jesus in Me is taken from
Colossians 1:9–10:

> *For this reason,*
>
> *since the day we heard about you,*
>
> *we have not stopped praying for you.*
>
> *We continually ask God to fill you with the knowledge of his will*
>
> *through all the wisdom and understanding that the Spirit gives,*
>
> *so that you may live a life worthy of the Lord and please him in every way:*
>
> *bearing fruit in every good work,*
>
> *growing in the knowledge of God . . .*

May God richly bless you as you continue to read your Bible, listening for His
voice.

Sincerely,

Anne

Write your own prayer of commitment here.

CONTENTS

THANK YOU   153

FOR STARTERS   155

SESSION 1: BIBLE STUDY WORKSHOP   159

SESSION 2: LOVING THE *Person* OF THE HOLY SPIRIT   161

SESSION 3: ENJOYING THE *Presence* OF THE HOLY SPIRIT   163

SESSION 4: RELYING ON THE *Power* OF THE HOLY SPIRIT   165

SESSION 5: EMBRACING THE *Purpose* OF THE HOLY SPIRIT   167

SESSION 6: LIVING BY THE *Precepts* OF THE HOLY SPIRIT   169

SESSION 7: REFLECTING THE *Purity* OF THE HOLY SPIRIT   171

SESSION 8: TRUSTING IN THE *Priority* OF THE HOLY SPIRIT   173

THANK YOU

THANK YOU FOR SERVING AS THE FACILITATOR for the participants who will join you in this study. While I will have the privilege of speaking to them through the video series, your leadership is essential. Your thoughtful and loving guidance will encourage them to consistently do their Bible study during the week and feel comfortable sharing their discoveries in your group. Please be assured that I, and others on this curriculum development team, have been praying for you.

I thank my God every time I remember you. In all my prayers for all of you,
I always pray with joy because of your partnership in the gospel from the first day until now, being
confident of this, that he who began a good work in you will carry it on to completion until the day of
Christ Jesus (Philippians 1:3–6).

As you lead others to discover the Holy Spirit as their constant companion, I pray that you will encourage each other to effectively share who the Holy Spirit is: Jesus in me. And in you.

For His Glory,

FOR STARTERS

P LEASE TAKE A FEW MINUTES to read this helpful information before you begin the *Jesus in Me* study. It should answer most of the questions you may have.

WHAT'S ON THE VIDEOS?

The accompanying videos feature the following components:

- An interactive workshop in session 1 led by Anne Graham Lotz that describes the Bible study method participants will be using.
- Seven additional video sessions with Anne that focus on learning about the Holy Spirit.

WHAT OTHER MATERIALS ARE NEEDED?

The following materials will be needed for a successful small group time:
- A computer with monitor, a television with a DVD player, or access to streaming video (see inside front cover)
- A watch, clock, or cellphone with alarm (to monitor the time)
- *Jesus in Me* Study Guide (one per group member)
- *Jesus in Me* Video Study (DVD or streaming video access, see inside front cover)
- A Bible (one per group member)
- Pens or pencils (enough for everyone)
- Optional: *Jesus in Me* book by Anne Graham Lotz (recommended for leaders, but optional for participants)

GOOD TO KNOW

Here are a few additional items to keep in mind as you lead your group:

- **Your Role as Facilitator:** As the facilitator, your role is to take care of your guests by managing the behind-the-scenes details so that when everyone arrives, they can just enjoy their time together. Your role is not to answer all the questions or reteach the content—the video and study guide will do much of the work. You want to guide the group and make it a place where people can process, question, and reflect on the Bible readings and the teachings.

- **Setting and Time:** This study can work equally well in church or home groups. The first session is planned to be 90 minutes in length, while the subsequent sessions are approximately 60 minutes. In more formal, time-sensitive church settings, you will likely need to follow the time frames provided in the session outline more closely in order to finish all the content. In less formal home settings, you can "round off" time frames and still end up with about an hour of study material. In either case, remember these are suggested time frames and are open to adjustment as you see fit.

- **Hospitality:** Regardless of where you conduct the study, create an environment that is conducive to sharing and learning. Make sure there is enough comfortable seating for everyone and, if possible, arrange the seats in a semicircle so everyone can see the video. This will make the transition between the video and group conversation more natural. Consider offering simple refreshments to create a welcoming atmosphere, and make sure your media technology is working properly before the session begins.

WEEKLY PREPARATION

As the facilitator, there are a few things you many want to do to prepare for each meeting:

- **Read through the lesson:** This will help you to become familiar with the content and know how to structure the discussion times.
- **Decide which questions you want to discuss:** You may not be able to cover every question in the group discussion section. Select the questions ahead of time that you absolutely want the group to discuss in depth.
- **Be familiar with the questions you want to discuss:** When the group meets you will be watching the clock, so make sure you are familiar with the study questions you have selected.
- **Pray for your group:** Pray for your group members by name throughout the week and ask God to lead them as they study His Word.
- **Bring extra supplies to your meeting:** The group members should bring their own pens for writing notes, but it's a good idea to have extras available for those who forget. You may also want to bring additional paper and Bibles.

GROUP DYNAMICS

Leading a group is highly rewarding, but that doesn't mean you will not encounter any challenges along the way. Discussions can get off track. Group members may not be sensitive to the ideas of others. Some may express comments that result in disagreements. To help ease this strain on you and the group, consider the following ground rules:

- **Off topic:** When someone raises a question or comment that is off the main topic, suggest you deal with it another time, or, if you feel led to go in that direction, let the group know you will be spending some time discussing it.
- **Don't know the answer:** If someone asks a question you don't know how to

answer, admit it and move on. At your discretion, feel free to invite group members to comment on questions that call for personal experience.

- **Dominating discussion:** If you find one or two people are dominating the discussion time, direct questions to others in the group. Outside the group time, ask the more dominating members to help you draw out the quieter ones. Work to make them a part of the solution instead of the problem.

- **Disagreements:** When a disagreement occurs, encourage group members to process the matter in love. Have those on opposite sides restate what they heard the other side say about the matter, and then invite each side to evaluate if that perception is accurate. It's most important that the answers given are based on the passages of Scripture studied.

When these situations arise, guide your group to follow the words from the Bible: "Love one another" (John 13:34), "As far as it depends on you, live at peace with everyone" (Romans 12:18), and "Be quick to listen, slow to speak and slow to become angry" (James 1:19).

BIBLE STUDY WORKSHOP

BIBLE STUDY WORKSHOP

For the best experience in facilitating this study, it's important to preview the video for session 1 and complete all the written exercises in this study guide prior to leading your group. Familiarize yourself with the session outline and gather the necessary materials. Pray for the participants by name (if known). Pray Ephesians 1:17–18 for them, that God will open their hearts to His Word and they will get to know Him better as a result of the Spirit's revelation.

SESSION OUTLINE (90 MINUTES)

I.   Introduction/Opening Prayer (5 minutes)

II. Explanation of Bible Study Sessions (5 minutes)

III. Video Teaching and Group Work (70 minutes)

    A.   Opening and Teaching on Steps 1–2 (13 minutes)

    B.   Group Work on Steps 1–2 (5 minutes)

    C.   Review of Steps 1–2 and Teaching on Step 3 (2 minutes)

    D.   Group Work on Step 3 (15 minutes)

    E.   Review of Step 3 and Teaching on Step 4 (13 minutes)

    F.   Group Work on Step 4 (5 minutes)

G. Review of Step 4 and Teaching on Step 5 (12 minutes)

H. Group Work on Step 5 (5 minutes)

IV. Wrapping Up and Next Steps (10 minutes)

INTRODUCTION/OPENING PRAYER (5 MINUTES)

Take a few moments as this opening session begins to introduce yourself to anyone in the group you do not know and give your contact information. If it can be done quickly, ask the participants to introduce themselves. It may be helpful in a larger group to provide nametags. To save time, you can have the nametags pre-printed with their names on one side, and your name and contact information on the other side. Ensure the participants have a copy of the study guide. Pray that God would use the coming hour to help everyone present to become more effective students and doers of His Word.

EXPLANATION OF BIBLE STUDY SESSIONS (5 MINUTES)

Explain that this first session in *Jesus in Me* is unique, as Anne will describe a method for studying the Bible that they will use during their personal quiet time throughout the study. During this opening session, which will be approximately 90 minutes in length, the group members will watch the video and complete the work found on pages 6–9.

VIDEO TEACHING AND GROUP WORK (70 MINUTES)

Show the video, following the instructions given by Anne during the session. Note that you will be stopping the video periodically for the participants to complete each of the steps.

WRAPPING UP AND NEXT STEPS (10 MINUTES)

Tell the group members that they will begin to explore the Holy Spirit in sessions 2–8. Refer group members to the Individual Bible Study found on page 11, and ask them to complete the studies before the next session. Close your time in prayer.

LOVING THE *Person* OF THE HOLY SPIRIT

Preview the video before your meeting and complete all the written exercises in this guide. Familiarize yourself with the session outline and gather the necessary materials. Remember also to pray for the participants who will be attending.

SESSION OUTLINE (60 MINUTES)

REVIEW OF PRE-SESSION BIBLE STUDY (15 MINUTES)

Welcome any new participants, and then refer the group to their notes on pages 14–24. As time allows, have one member share the facts he or she drew from each verse (Step 2). Then have several different members share the following:

- The lessons they learned from each verse (Step 3).
- The most meaningful question they wrote out in response to Step 4, citing the verse on which the question was based.
- Their outstanding takeaway in Step 5.

VIDEO TEACHING (18 MINUTES)

Watch the teaching video for session 2. Refer the group members to page 27 and remind them there is space to take notes.

GROUP DISCUSSION (17 MINUTES)

Refer to the Group Discussion questions on page 28 to stimulate discussion on the topics presented during the video teaching. Ask the group members to share any personal encouragement, challenge, or inspiration they received as they watched.

WRAP UP AND GO DEEPER (10 MINUTES)

Conclude by praying over your group. Review the next week's schedule on page 32 and finally close your group meeting by reading the blessing and encouragement on page 29. Remind them to read the passage and complete the studies before the next session. Close in prayer.

ENJOYING THE *Presence* OF THE HOLY SPIRIT

P REVIEW THE VIDEO BEFORE YOUR MEETING and complete all the written exercises in this guide. Familiarize yourself with the session outline and gather the necessary materials. Remember also to pray for the participants who will be attending.

SESSION OUTLINE (60 MINUTES)

REVIEW OF PRE-SESSION BIBLE STUDY (15 MINUTES)

Welcome any new participants, and then refer the group to their notes on pages 34–44. As time allows, have one member share the facts he or she drew from each verse (Step 2). Then have several different members share the following:

- The lessons they learned from each verse (Step 3).
- The most meaningful question they wrote out in response to Step 4, citing the verse on which the question was based.
- Their outstanding takeaway in Step 5.

VIDEO TEACHING (17:30 MINUTES)

Watch the teaching video for session 3. Refer the group members to the outline on page 47 and remind them there is space to take notes.

GROUP DISCUSSION (17 MINUTES)

Refer to the Group Discussion questions on page 48 to stimulate discussion on the topics presented during the video teaching. Ask the group members to share any personal encouragement, challenge, or inspiration they received as they watched.

WRAP UP AND GO DEEPER (10 MINUTES)

Conclude by praying over your group. Review the next week's schedule on page 52 and finally close your group meeting by reading the blessing and encouragement on page 49. Remind them to read the passage and complete the studies before the next session. Close in prayer.

RELYING ON THE
Power OF THE HOLY SPIRIT

PREVIEW THE VIDEO BEFORE YOUR MEETING and complete all the written exercises in this guide. Familiarize yourself with the session outline and gather the necessary materials. Remember also to pray for the participants who will be attending.

SESSION OUTLINE (60 MINUTES)

REVIEW OF PRE-SESSION BIBLE STUDY (15 MINUTES)

Welcome any new participants, and then refer the group to their notes on pages 54–64. As time allows, have one member share the facts he or she drew from each verse (Step 2). Then have several different members share the following:

- The lessons they learned from each verse (Step 3).
- The most meaningful question they wrote out in response to Step 4, citing the verse on which the question was based.
- Their outstanding takeaway in Step 5.

VIDEO TEACHING (17 MINUTES)

Watch the teaching video for session 4. Refer the group members to page 67 and remind them there is space to take notes.

GROUP DISCUSSION (17 MINUTES)

Refer to the Group Discussion questions on page 68 to stimulate discussion on the topics presented during the video teaching. Ask the group members to share any personal encouragement, challenge, or inspiration they received as they watched.

WRAP UP AND GO DEEPER (10 MINUTES)

Conclude by praying over your group. Review the next week's schedule on page 72 and finally close your group meeting by reading the blessing and encouragement on page 69. Remind them to read the passage and complete the studies before the next session. Close in prayer.

EMBRACING THE
Purpose OF THE HOLY SPIRIT

PREVIEW THE VIDEO BEFORE YOUR MEETING and complete all the written exercises in this guide. Familiarize yourself with the session outline and gather the necessary materials. Remember also to pray for the participants who will be attending.

SESSION OUTLINE (60 MINUTES)

REVIEW OF PRE-SESSION BIBLE STUDY (15 MINUTES)

Welcome any new participants, and then refer the group to their notes on pages 74–84. As time allows, have one member share the facts he or she drew from each verse (Step 2). Then have several different members share the following:

- The lessons they learned from each verse (Step 3).
- The most meaningful question they wrote out in response to Step 4, citing the verse on which the question was based.
- Their outstanding takeaway in Step 5.

VIDEO TEACHING (15 MINUTES)

Watch the teaching video for session 5. Refer the group members to page 87 and remind them there is space to take notes.

GROUP DISCUSSION (17 MINUTES)

Refer to the Group Discussion questions on page 88 to stimulate discussion on the topics presented during the video teaching. Ask the group members to share any personal encouragement, challenge, or inspiration they received as they watched.

WRAP UP AND GO DEEPER (10 MINUTES)

Conclude by praying over your group. Review the next week's schedule on page 92 and finally close your group meeting by reading the blessing and encouragement on page 89. Remind them to read the passage and complete the studies before the next session. Close in prayer.

LIVING BY THE
Precepts OF THE HOLY SPIRIT

PREVIEW THE VIDEO BEFORE YOUR MEETING and complete all the written exercises in this guide. Familiarize yourself with the session outline and gather the necessary materials. Remember also to pray for the participants who will be attending.

SESSION OUTLINE (60 MINUTES)

REVIEW OF PRE-SESSION BIBLE STUDY (15 MINUTES)

Welcome any new participants, and then refer the group to their notes on pages 94–104. As time allows, have one member share the facts he or she drew from each verse (Step 2). Then have several different members share the following:

- The lessons they learned from each verse (Step 3).
- The most meaningful question they wrote out in response to Step 4, citing the verse on which the question was based.
- Their outstanding takeaway in Step 5.

VIDEO TEACHING (16:30 MINUTES)

Watch the teaching video for session 6. Refer the group members to the outline on page 107 and remind them there is space to take notes.

GROUP DISCUSSION (17 MINUTES)

Refer to the Group Discussion questions on page 108 to stimulate discussion on the topics presented during the video teaching. Ask the group members to share any personal encouragement, challenge, or inspiration they received as they watched.

WRAP UP AND GO DEEPER (10 MINUTES)

Conclude by praying over your group. Review the next week's schedule on page 112 and finally close your group meeting by reading the blessing and encouragement on page 109. Remind them to read the passage and complete the studies before the next session. Close in prayer.

REFLECTING THE *Purity* OF THE HOLY SPIRIT

PREVIEW THE VIDEO BEFORE YOUR MEETING and complete all the written exercises in this guide. Familiarize yourself with the session outline and gather the necessary materials. Remember also to pray for the participants who will be attending.

SESSION OUTLINE (60 MINUTES)

REVIEW OF PRE-SESSION BIBLE STUDY (15 MINUTES)

Welcome any new participants, and then refer the group to their notes on pages 114–124. As time allows, have one member share the facts he or she drew from each verse (Step 2). Then have several different members share the following:

- The lessons they learned from each verse (Step 3).
- The most meaningful question they wrote out in response to Step 4, citing the verse on which the question was based.
- Their outstanding takeaway in Step 5.

VIDEO TEACHING (16:30 MINUTES)

Watch the teaching video for session 7. Refer the group members to page 127 and remind them there is space to take notes.

GROUP DISCUSSION (17 MINUTES)

Refer to the Group Discussion questions on page 128 to stimulate discussion on the topics presented during the video teaching. Ask the group members to share any personal encouragement, challenge, or inspiration they received as they watched.

WRAP UP AND GO DEEPER (10 MINUTES)

Conclude by praying over your group. Review the next week's schedule on page 132 and finally close your group meeting by reading the blessing and encouragement on page 129. Remind them to read the passage and complete the studies before the next session. Close in prayer.

TRUSTING IN THE
Priority OF THE HOLY SPIRIT

Preview the video before your meeting and complete all the written exercises in this guide. Familiarize yourself with the session outline and gather the necessary materials. Remember also to pray for the participants who will be attending.

SESSION OUTLINE (60 MINUTES)

REVIEW OF PRE-SESSION BIBLE STUDY (15 MINUTES)

Welcome any new participants, and then refer the group to their notes on pages 134–144. As time allows, have one member share the facts he or she drew from each verse (Step 2). Then have several different members share the following:

- The lessons they learned from each verse (Step 3).
- The most meaningful question they wrote out in response to Step 4, citing the verse on which the question was based.
- Their outstanding takeaway in Step 5.

VIDEO TEACHING (21:30 MINUTES)

Watch the teaching video for session 8. Refer the group members to page 132 and remind them there is space to take notes.

GROUP DISCUSSION (17 MINUTES)

Refer to the Group Discussion questions on page 148 to stimulate discussion on the topics presented during the video teaching. Ask the group members to share any personal encouragement, challenge, or inspiration they received as they watched.

WRAP UP AND GO DEEPER (10 MINUTES)

Conclude by praying over your group. Take the opportunity to meet again soon to discuss some of the new things the Holy Spirit is teaching you.

Pray too for each other to effectively share with people outside the group about who the Holy Spirit is: Jesus in me. And in you.

BIBLE STUDY
SOURCE
for women
powered by ChurchSource

Connecting you with the best in

BIBLE STUDY RESOURCES

from many of the world's

MOST TRUSTED BIBLE TEACHERS

| JENNIE ALLEN | JADA EDWARDS | ANNE GRAHAM LOTZ | CHRYSTAL EVANS HURST |

Providing

WOMEN'S MINISTRY AND SMALL GROUP LEADERS

with the INSPIRATION, ENCOURAGEMENT, AND RESOURCES to grow your ministry

powered by ChurchSource

join our
COMMUNITY

Use our BIBLE STUDY FINDER to quickly find the perfect study for your group, learn more about all the new studies available, and download FREE printables to help you make the most of your Bible study experience.

BibleStudySourceForWomen.com